VIBE

THE SOUND AND FEELING OF BLACK LIFE
IN THE AMERICAN SOUTH

COREY J. MILES

University Press of Mississippi / Jackson

Publication of this book was made possible in part by support from the Tulane University School of Liberal Arts.

Margaret Walker Alexander Series in African American Studies

The University Press of Mississippi is the scholarly publishing agency of the Mississippi Institutions of Higher Learning: Alcorn State University, Delta State University, Jackson State University, Mississippi State University, Mississippi University for Women, Mississippi Valley State University, University of Mississippi, and University of Southern Mississippi.

www.upress.state.ms.us

Frontis image by Todgi Dozier

The University Press of Mississippi is a member of the Association of University Presses.

Library of Congress Cataloging-in-Publication Data

Names: Miles, Corey J., author.
Title: Vibe : the sound and feeling of Black life in the American South / Corey J. Miles.
Other titles: Sound and feeling of Black life in the American South | Margaret Walker Alexander series in African American studies.
Description: Jackson : University Press of Mississippi, [2023] | Series: Margaret Walker Alexander series in African American studies | Includes bibliographical references and index.
Identifiers: LCCN 2023028659 (print) | LCCN 2023028660 (ebook) | ISBN 9781496847287 (hardback) | ISBN 9781496848901 (trade paperback) | ISBN 9781496847294 (epub) | ISBN 9781496847300 (epub) | ISBN 9781496847317 (pdf) | ISBN 9781496847324 (pdf)
Subjects: LCSH: African Americans—Southern States—Social conditions. | African Americans—Race identity—Southern States. | African Americans—Music—History and criticism. | Trap (Music)—Social aspects—Southern States. | Trap (Music)—Political aspects—Southern States. | Hip-hop—Social aspects—Southern States. | Hip-hop—Political aspects—Southern States.
Classification: LCC E185.92 .M55 2023 (print) | LCC E185.92 (ebook) | DDC 975.08996/073—dc23/eng/20230712
LC record available at https://lccn.loc.gov/2023028659
LC ebook record available at https://lccn.loc.gov/2023028660

British Library Cataloging-in-Publication Data available

we loved and laughed
as mother and son
not even death can change that

The situation in Alabama and Mississippi which is spectacular and surprises the country is nationwide. Not only could it happen in Florida, it could happen in New York or Chicago, Detroit or anywhere there's a significant Negro population. Because until today, all the Negroes in this country in one way or another, in different fashions, North and South, are kept in what is, in effect, prison. In the North, one lives in ghettos and in the South, the situation is so intolerable as to become sinister not only for Mississippi or Alabama or Florida but for the whole future of this country.
—JAMES BALDWIN

CONTENTS

PRELUDE

I'm lost.

When I decided to go home, I needed to figure out where it was. Not that I didn't know how to get there, but I didn't know how to tell a story about where it was situated. The 252 (pronounced 2–5–2) area code is in northeast North Carolina at the uppermost tip of the Black Belt. It's up South. I grew up Black, rural, and southern.

"Nigga, that ain't the real South," a brother from Alabama once told me.

His challenge of my southernness assumed that if it ain't Deep South, it ain't South. It never crossed his mind that there may be multiple Souths. Honestly it didn't cross mine either until I started looking for where the South was at.

I wanted to find the South.

I wanted to find that place that gave my insides a semblance of identity and belonging.

That brother from Alabama was more honest than he knew. North Carolina isn't the real South. It's *a* South. What I mean by this is that it is one of the geographical spaces that complement and complicate how we imagine where the South in the United States is and what happens there.

Finding the South is complicated. White folks have added to this difficulty. They see the South differently than I do. They imagine there is a distance between where the South is today and where it was in the past. They believe it has moved on from what made it possible to begin with. That was violence. There could be no US expansion without the enslaving of African people. Without the stealing of Native land in the North and West, we would not consider the South the South. We know where the South is in part because of where we look when we are comparing it.

I came back home concerned about this. This is not just a question of geography, but one of both space and time. I wanted to know where the South is at physically. Maps lie, though. They make the South too rigid. Maps don't account for its curves and its choreography. They don't capture the moments, sounds, and feelings that make a South possible. Also, locating the South is to situate it temporally. Taken-for-granted assumptions have forced many people in this country to believe that we left the *Old* South behind. Progress myths have moved the region further from the past than it is.

This is why I need to find the South. To find the South is to locate the experiences, noises, silences, movements, feelings, and memories that make something that we call South possible. It requires paying attention to the softest and hardest parts of people whose insides hold the South even when their physical body isn't there. It requires being still, dancing, listening, yelling, and being in the South. You have to vibe with the South to get a glimpse of where it is at.

I hear and feel the South in various places. I hear it in the slamming of kitchen cabinets. It reminds me of the way my mama curls her syllables when she yells at me for "tearing her kitchen up." I feel it in the ridges of my fingers. When I rub my hand across my skin, I feel the softness of skin that had the privilege not to do physical labor. My grandma's hands were rough. The small circles in her fingers carried the weight of working manual-labor jobs that never paid enough for her to afford to go out for a cooked meal. She worked after her shift was over.

I hear the South the most, or at least well enough to write about, in trap music. The grittiness and heaviness of the drums hit the body like the despair that fills the air of a region that can't be honest about itself. The racial and economic tension of the South pounds and tries to break through the lies that we use to cover the ugliness of the South. The unruly lyrics about guns and drugs capture the desperation, despair, and desire of the region. Women and men willing to risk what little life and freedom they have, to get at least one of the unfulfilled promises of America. Trap music is southern Black music. Which means it is America's music.

To feel and hear the South, I need to go to where trap music is. I need to sit with the experiences of those who came of age in the South in the trap music era. Just as blues is more than music, it is a way of making sense of the world. I want to use the sound, feeling, and choreography of trap to make sense of where the South is at right now. Trap is how those who have experienced the worst of the South make sense of the country. Those whose mobility is limited to making the most out of choices that aren't really choices. The heaviness of the sound carries our grief, anger, and pain. By focusing on those who have experienced the worst of the South, we get to see how despite the terribleness of the region people continuously decide to stay and to carry the South with them if they do leave.

Those who are honest about the horrifying parts of a place can better appreciate the beautiful pieces. Pain pares down to the essence of an experience. It makes details clearer, even the ones that live beneath the surface. There is red clay in North Carolina. You would know that only if you spent enough time there to get dirty.

Trap brings us to moments of impact, moments of violence. It is in these moments that we feel what we have, what we have lost, and what we have been denied. In this way trap is Black life. It is how Black people in the South and beyond make sense of, survive, and subvert an impossible and deathly reality.

To get closer to the South I needed to get closer to this sound.

I needed to feel the red clay. Sit near the softest parts of people who had a hard life. I wanted to vibe with what was under the surface because I always believed the South was down there somewhere.

VIBE

The 2-5-2

Premo starts to sip his drink rather than taking swigs. The slow burn of the liquor begins making our conversation more intimate. It drowns out the other folks at the bar and makes our words come out a little more honest than sober us would have anticipated. Early in our conversation, Premo, only twenty-six years old, sounded hopeful about his music career. After the whisky loosened our grip on the pieces of our insides that we like to hold tight, his voice began to sound more like the bar we were in. It started to make space for multiple truths.

"So, we getting in our feelings tonight," he says.

I look around this chain restaurant that has basketball on big-screen TVs and random sports pictures on the wall and wonder if anything honest can be spoken in here. Nothing about this place speaks to Greenville, the city we met up in. Black folks began to filter in between our laughs and improvised raps. As the night went on, it started to feel like we were supposed to be here. While most locally owned spots are full of white folks, Black people gather at the chain bars and restaurants to drink, eat bland appetizers, and trash-talk with and to each other. It is often the way Black folks relate, love, and give each other space to disagree that makes a space feel like theirs, even when a space wasn't built for them.

Prior to reaching out to Premo via Facebook, I questioned how to introduce myself in a way that could hold the intricacy of who I was at that moment. While I am from the 252 (pronounced 2–5–2), the area code in northeast North Carolina that encompasses thirty mainly rural counties, with Greenville being one of the largest cities, not too many of us low-income Black folk who call this place home go pursue PhDs.

"You good with them books," my family and community members always recited to me. "Good with them books" didn't inherently mean smart, but it assumed I could wield and perform knowledge in ways that would allow me to be successful, or at least survive, in a white world.[1] I didn't want my being good with books to create a conceptual and emotional distance between Premo and me, as it did in my earlier life when community members felt they had to perform more tempered versions of their selves with me.

It ain't no public transportation in the 252. Folks either drive or borrow rides. Early 2016, I can't recall the month, a family member sent me a link to Premo's SoundCloud, and I waited until the next time I took a ride to play it, because music feels different when you hear the bass vibrating on the car's dashboard. Four lines into the first track by Premo I ever heard, he flows, "Bad blood on my hands / For us to eat I caused the bleeding." As I road on a quiet back road early morning, I made a stank face while bobbing with a little more bounce in my neck to that line even though I didn't really know what it meant. But its opacity hit me in my chest. Maybe he was referencing moments he engaged in behavior that strained his familial relationships but was acting in the best way he knew possible to survive the precariousness of Black life. I sat with the imagery it created of sacrificing both morally and physically one's own being to support those we claim to care for. It is something about struggle that reveals our commitments. I never asked about what that line meant; I was more interested in what that line did to me. Premo's music made me feel pain and love, and I wanted to understand the person who could make me *feel*.

To lean on the closeness we developed through discussing the many ways we were connected through hip-hop, I ask Premo about his childhood growing up in the 252.

"I was a typical kid. I went to school, played sports, was a little popular, and had a few run-ins with the law," Premo tells me.

His brief statement paired with the matter-of-fact disposition to the notion that having run-ins with law enforcement was part of a typical childhood captures many of the sentiments of the rural Black people in the 252 that I worked with between 2016 and 2020. Even as a Black boy who was good with them books, I had my own stories of run-ins with law enforcement. Police contact as a defining feature of Black life in rural towns underscored the community's understanding of what the South was and where it was at.

"What happened with the run-ins?" I ask, trying not to pry too deeply.

He sits up straight and softly says, "Doing dumb stuff, which I shouldn't have. Because even when we aren't doing anything, cops make us [Black people] feel some type of way." As Premo and I talked that night, a lot of the conversation centered on hip-hop and our anxieties, but mentally I kept returning to this statement that cops made Black people feel some type of way. As a Black boy from the South, I too recognized my unsettledness around police officers, particularly in my first traffic stop during my field-work, where I responded to the officer with less of my southern cadence and more of the language I developed from being good with books. With the cop I thought if I could say something that sounded structured and thoughtful, like the words on these pages, then value could be seen in me.

In this book I consider how emotions are racialized and the ways Black people "get in their feelings," or work through emotions to make sense of where they are at. With the South serving as the seat of race in the United States, dominant understandings of the South often foreclose the possibility of engaging with the emotional complexity of the region. To make space for the region in a postracial America, the country has had to hide the grief, pain, and anger that chain together Black folks' memories and experiences of the South. Imani Perry has called this a convenient misunderstanding of the South's choreography and rhythm.[2] I am not immediately interested in getting the United States in formation or on beat, but rather in excavating the experiences of Black southerners who came of age in the trap music era to examine the ways they use feeling and unfeeling to come to know and communicate where the South is and where they are located within it.[3]

Just ask anyone from the South who has a had a Black grandma love on them, and they will tell you that communication isn't really what is said but is about the way a person's head slightly tilts to the side while talking, and how instructions often don't make us feel like we know anything new but that we should have known better. Meaning is in the way a message is given, the aesthetics of it. Exploring the inner lives of southern trap artists like Premo looks beyond what is said to the poetics, bodily movements, and rhythm of Black life to understand the South.

Trap music is a gritty sound. This is largely due to the hi-hats, 808s, and crime-and-drug lyrical structure that organizes the genre. Premo using trap music to move people to feel the pain of struggling in the rural South and his ability to make chain restaurants feel like home both speak to the ways the inner lives of Black people can shift spatial, cultural, and symbolic boundaries of exclusion.[4] The emotional is tied to the material. Premo helped me feel this.

"My boy, you have a good vibe," Premo tells me. "You are doing something important for the community."

The left corner of my mouth curves into a smile. "I appreciate that," I say as I am pulling cash out of my wallet to leave a tip.

Initially, I took Premo's statement as him commenting on my personality, believing that he assumed I was sincere. Maybe the way I performed care for our area code made him think that I would enact change. When saying goodbye, we dapped each other up with the right hand and hugged with the other. I felt something in our embrace. It felt like when two Black boys find comfort in each other through the few acceptable ways that Black boys are allowed to touch each other in the South.

Care is relational.

In that hug I rethought my initial understanding of what Premo meant by vibe and was moving to think he was making less an evaluation about my personality than an analysis about a type of experience with me. Vibe is relational. It is the aura and social climate produced when ideas, people, and spaces collide. It is the sensation that lets us know history is sitting in the room with us, even the pieces we were denied access to. Premo and I had just bonded through holding similar fears and anxieties about the carceral system, and the texture of how we related was altered. It wasn't that I would go on to do good for the community, but that we were constructing something in that moment. Vibe works to name the often unsayable and perceptive ways Black people know, feel, and respond to the opacity and unquantifiable dimensions of social experiences.

There are two points being made here. The first is that emotions help southern Black people build understanding of space. Premo and other 252 artists work within the trap music genre—which is a southern hip-hop tradition that was popularized in Atlanta and whose content centers on dealing drugs layered over triple-time subdivided hi-hats, heavy sub-bass, and kick drums—to negotiate emotional subjectivity.[5] Its lyrics center on crime, drugs, and guns, but the sonic experience produces a moment to sit with pain, grief, love, and a host of other emotions that encompass the day-to-day experience of being Black in the rural South. The other point here is that vibe names the process in which Black southerners use the felt experience of their social location to understand social structures, and it is a linguistic device used by southern Black folks to communicate the ways our senses are alert to how the historical, biographical, and material structure experience. Emotions have a good memory. Vibe is a perceptual, political, and affective tool that attempts to capture ways macro-level processes make themselves felt and known in the day-to-day lives of Black people.

Premo and I vibed well in part because a lot of our pain and fragileness was due to the criminal legal system. We hurt in common. His relationship with the carceral system was different than mine, though. He had been formally processed and has a retrievable record that documents the conditions in which he was pulled into the system. Beyond a speeding ticket, I have no formal criminal record or experiences with the criminal legal system that will show up in any database. My experience escapes quantifiable ways of understanding the carceral state and doesn't show up in the numbers of millions of people incarcerated and under other forms of correctional control. But Premo and I bonded through the ways we both came to understand the precariousness of Black life through the carceral system.

To understand Premo's and my connection, there needs to be an accounting for the ways anti-Blackness, often organized within the criminal legal system, impacts all Black people in ways that complicate the binary of either being under correctional control or not. What does it look and feel like to move past understanding Black life through numerical calculations of disparity, or what Kathrine McKittrick calls "the mathematics of the unliving," and take seriously the unsayable and unindexed sounds, feelings, and moments that make up Black life?[6] I'm trying to get y'all to vibe with me. Vibe is a mode of making sense of relational processes in ways that push back against rationalistic and objective ways of knowing to make room for the possibility that something important can occur absent of us being able to develop a language to approximate that experience.[7]

While Premo was making a valuation of me based on my vibe, whether that assessment was right or wrong, he was conducting a similar reading of his relationship with the criminal legal system. Premo reading my vibe points to ways Black people in the American South and beyond have constructed their own epistemological understandings of the world that rely on Black subjectivity.[8] My use of "South" here in one way is a geographical reference to the sites of chattel slavery and Jim Crow, but in another way I use it as an incomplete frame that works through how the American imagery has positioned the South as a conceptual space for a specific style of racialized experience and how that experience has broader implications that transgress region.

Premo's use of "feel some type of way," essentially vibe, to make sense of his racialized relationship to space echoes the voice of Zora Neale Hurston and how she captured the performative and affective economics of race.[9] In *How Does It Feel to Be Colored Me*, Hurston narrates growing up in the rural South and that before she consciously felt her race that white people differed from colored only in that they rode through town and never lived there. Even as a child who hadn't yet come to feel the full weight of Blackness, Hurston knew that race was about space. It was about movement. It informed who had places to go and armed them with the ability to trespass anyone's space to get there. Just as Hurston came to know herself as colored in heart and mirror, Premo and other southern Black folk knew Blackness and its relationship to the South through feeling. Feeling some type of way references a bodily feeling or sensation that extends beyond and overwhelms one's emotional vocabulary. It is when someone doesn't have the language to make sense of what they feel and those times when someone is unsure about their feelings but know they are feeling something.

In the South, Black people feel a lot more than they can and have been allowed to say. Despite these limits they have used peculiar sensations to help make sense of their social location and to move accordingly.[10] Vibe, then, is grounded in the ways Black southerners have routinely made sense of the world through working at the intersections of the empirical, spiritual, and emotive. Looking at the American South and beyond from this frame uncovers invisible realities and geographies or, as southern writer Kiese Laymon says, "gives us a different relationship to honesty."[11] When Premo and others use "feel" some type of way, it is because they have complex emotional realties that are difficult to communicate, and their desires, emotions, and intentions are not as one-dimensional as folks who benefit from their criminalization would like us to believe.

FEELING SOME TYPE OF WAY

The 252 is big, but it's not. It spans thirty rural counties. The population is slightly over a million, and people are spread across 226 cities (towns), with cities having as few as six hundred residents. You must drive everywhere, and in car rides the fields you pass often remind you of the tobacco and cotton slave plantations that were once here, largely due to the fact Black people in the area still don't make any money off that land. When slavery died businesses and people from the 252 migrated north and west, and the constant outmigration has continued through today.[12]

Who remain in these counties are Black people who live in the spatial shadow of slavery. Just as Premo and I could make chain restaurants like Carolina Ale House feel like ours, Black people have found ways to feel at home here. They have stomped their feet while catching the Holy Ghost enough times on this brown soil to know that there is red clay under. While living in the "afterlife of slavery" on lands reddened by the sweat and blood of their ancestors, Black folks have felt intimacy here enough to know that there is more to Black life in the area than what is on the surface.[13] *Vibe* is a story about Black feeling serving as a method to understand and name the South, but beneath that brown soil is red clay, which is a narrative about placemaking. Just as clay can be soft or hard, build structures, and adapt, Black feeling can be strategically used to create "sites of endurance, belonging, and resistance" within dark structures.[14]

It is about noon on a weekday, and I am leaving my apartment in Halifax County to get on Highway 95 to head to Greenville to talk with Nicole. If you roll your windows down and drive slow enough, you can hear crickets in the trees making music to fill the emptiness of the air. Most folks are at work, typically in a local factory. There is a sour smell from the local paper mill that fills the air, which I eventually grew (re)accustomed to. This smell represented a community member's livelihood, their ability to feed their family in a county that has been disinvested in by the state government. In southern rural counties with high Black populations, or what Harin Contractor and Spencer Overton call the "Black rural South," work is hard to come by and often comes with a foul odor and air that makes you cough a little harder than usual.[15] Air has a good memory.

In the eight-minute drive from my apartment to the highway, I pass three Dollar Generals. A month from now, Stacie will be pulled over by police officers outside the second Dollar General. Sometime between when I left the 252 and when I returned, these dollar stores became an intimate part of the South.

I remember my drive to Nicole differently because of Stacie. I feel different writing about this moment than I did during it, because now I know what happens here in the future. Stacie's story is a different story than Nicole's, but to tell one sincerely, I must tell them together. This is what Eddie Glaude Jr. means when he says that pain fragments how we remember.[16] A month after my drive to Nicole, Stacie will be pulled over beside this building that is two shades of brown with a bright yellow sign on it that lets you know it's a dollar store even before your eyes can make out the actual shape of the building. Stacie, a twenty-nine-year-old resident, would often call me to chat about things going on in the 252 that she thought I needed to know. On this Thursday evening, I'm going to get a call from Stacie, and upon my answering she is going to immediately start talking quickly. Not fast in an anxious way, but it seemed like if she paused between her words, that would let out a cry that she wouldn't be able to put back in. She had to say it all before the tears consumed her.

She is going to get pulled over for what she contends was using her asthma pump while driving. The cop is going to stop her and ask about an unknown object that she will be holding while having only one hand on the wheel.

Speaking in a rhythm where her voice deflates at the end of her sentences to catch her breath, she is going to tell me, "It's an asthma pump." She acts the scene out over the phone for me.

"The way he looked at me I felt like I had a gun, but he said he wanted to make sure I wasn't texting and driving." Opening the conversation for me to join, she is going to ask, "Was this racist?"

During my pause to collect my thoughts, Stacie will sobbingly say, "I just wanted to make it home to my mama. I should have went off on him, though."

As I am putting myself mentally back in the day of Stacie's story, now I know that in two years George Floyd will call out for his late mother as he is dying, and Daunte Wright will call his mother upon being pulled over, right before he is killed. When Stacie called that day, I didn't yet have those stories as references when trying to answer her question. I hadn't yet made the connection between traffic stops and the way Black mamas care for us when we have been undone.

Despite not having the language to make sense of her encounter as legally racist, I knew Stacie deserved more than what I was equipped to offer. The ways Black people are made unfree often work well within the South's current juridical organization. I provided Stacie with a faulty response, so much so that I do not want to quote it here, and we were both forced to sit with Kathrine McKittrick's plea that "a story cannot tell itself without our willingness to imagine what it cannot tell."[17] That moment was powerful because we didn't know what it meant. Stacie felt some type of way, so she knew that it mattered. Neither one of us knew if she should take some form or legal action or the best way to move forward from the experience. But we both knew those moments mattered, in ways more important than juridical conclusions. She survived physically whole, but something was broken.

I felt worthless.

The vibe of that moment did a type of violence that is not easily sayable. Vibe engages with the messiness of anti-Blackness, the ways that we experience it not just objectively, but emotionally. It forces us to sit with the unknowable when our bodies are telling us that *something* is occurring. Vibe has been theorized by scholars as emotional resonance and as a communicative tool used to transmit and perceive intuitive signals.[18] I may be taking Du Bois too literally. But vibe seems to be a way to sincerely approximate the souls of southern Black folk. To tell us something about the way our insides fold to protect themselves. How that thing deep down within us knows what the South is. This allows us to understand where Black people are located within the South, because as Eduardo Bonilla-Silva suggests, Black people can feel the structural weight of their location within the social order.[19] Black feeling allows us to re- and un-map spaces and memories. Pain forces memories to rupture and collide. This why I couldn't get to Nicole without sitting with Stacie.

The reason I passed so many dollar stores to get to Nicole and why it was likely Stacie was pulled over in front of one speaks to the development of this region postslavery. Agricultural slavery was prominent in the 252, and the end of slavery killed the economic lifeblood and the identity of the region, with industrialization and banking taking shape in the western part of the state in cities such as Charlotte. Black folks who remained in the 252 advocated for landownership but were undermined by the racism that fortifies big business. By the 1970s Black landownership in the 252 was on the decline due to the emergence of agribusiness and continued discriminatory practices by the Farm Homeowners Association within the USDA.[20] Those who own the land here don't live here. Dollar stores, waste dumps, and paper mills are always attracted to poor rural Black towns.

When I met Nicole at a chicken wing spot in Greenville, I first noticed her arm tattoos and how pretty smiles can make men both nervous and comfortable. The place was small and colorful. It had a familial vibe. Maybe this was because only one other customer was there besides us. He swirled slowly on his barstool while smiling, laughing, and yelling with the person behind the bar the entire time we were there. Black conversations don't really feel friendly unless you can get a little loud with the other person. Nicole is a local artist and alopecia survivor and contends that her alopecia adds flava to her music, because dealing with hair loss brings in a layer of vulnerability to her sound that people vibe with.[21]

Looking out the glass door past the empty parking lot to an emptier shopping center across the street, I ask, "Are you from around here?"

"Yes. I'm from near here, right by Greenville," she says. "I've been here most of my life, but I moved a few times, and I came back. I said this the last time because when I move again, I ain't coming back to the hood, it's rough round here."

There was honesty in her words. In these rural towns, people respond to the question "Where are you from?" with a large city that is near their town, because they know that small rural places don't exist in most folks' mental maps. Maps are problematic anyway. They locate the hood in the urban centers of major cities. Just look for the streets named after Black people that white folks didn't like until they were dead. That's where maps say the hood is. Hearing Nicole, whose vowels are longer than the empty parking lot outside, talk about being from the hood repositions where it is located. Nicole and other rural Black southerners may exist outside of urban centers, but they don't live outside of concentrated poverty, surveillance, policing, and other structural processes that are assumed to unfold in the hood. The rural and urban overlap, or, as John Easton's interlocutor says, "It's the same, only quieter."[22] The hood can be southern, rural, and quiet—it's more mobile than we were led to believe.

Nicole started singing as a young child in the church choir, because her grandmother encouraged her to be active. Now she uses her music to connect with and inspire Black women and men locally. "What are things you want people to understand about you and your community?" I ask halfway through our conversation. Nicole states:

> I feel like with the police brutality it's one of the biggest things. You cut on the TV, and you can see a Black person dead. It happens round here too, even though they don't want to talk about it happening in small towns, but we know it do. It's not even just that they killing us, but that nobody even cares or know when they do.

Greenville's crime rate per 100,000 people is 32 percent above the national average.[23] This justifies that the rural Black South is heavily policed. Not that it needs justification. Policing's roots are rural and southern.[24] Avoiding police on the grounds that your enslaved ancestors were patrolled on is difficult work. It requires an attention to detail. For Nicole, the racialized impact of police brutality in rural spaces is exacerbated through the ways small rural areas are often erased from how we imagine where and when police violence occurs. Drop, Elijah, Corey. Names of rural Black people that have been victims of unjust policing. Friend, Brother, Self. Their relationship to me. We know the stories. But there isn't a large-scale system of accounting to understand the nuances of carceral practices in the rural South.

The structural disregarding and erasure of violence toward Black people in the rural South is part of a long history of telling static one-dimensional stories about the South to make room for it in the United States' imagined history. On one hand, this imagined history says racism is harsher in the South and not indicative of the rest of the country. On the other, racism in the South is linked to bigots, not how systems are organized. Racism is a product of backward white folks who don't represent America. These two taken together disarm us from seeing the likely connection that the people who live on the grounds in which policing was born have an intimate relationship with law enforcement.

Nicole is a living witness to this alchemy. To not have the violence you face recognized as such is violent. Our modes of attending to each other must be precise. In the South to gauge how one needs to be cared for, we rarely ask them "What do you feel?" but generally ask "How do you feel?" In this regard I am concerned with how Black people feel and the epistemological possibilities created as a result. "How" points to a process, a way of being and doing. Tracing the "how" of feeling is to be concerned with a type of politic used, by those who weren't considered human, to transform fractured memories, bodily sensations, felt moments, and intuition into an economy of thought and knowing.

Nicole and others know that carceral violence has been a defining feature of the rural Black experience even when the South's interpretations of itself don't say so. I'm searching for the type of memory and felt experiences that equipped soul-trap rapper Rod Wave to say, "I ain't been home in two weeks, I been looking for peace," in the face of a society whose normative understanding is that homes and families are sites of refuge. Some people have had to run away to get toward something that felt like freedom. I think Rod Wave knew this. While Black people are often thought of as what Jennifer Tilton calls "emotional suspects," they have felt and known the world in ways that challenge simplistic understandings of place.[25] Southern people be in their feelings a lot.

Being in the 252 where I grew up, and sitting in conversations with folks like Nicole, I often felt at home. Maybe, this is my feelings telling me something. That every time I have an honest exchange with someone about the place I call home, it is always filled with various ways the people I am committed to feel harmed by this place. Home seems to always deal with origin, familiarity, and dependability, but pain can be all of those too. In this version of home, I was at least close to family. I had people I could be still with.

On a Friday evening, I was headed to the store to grab a few things before I had to get ready for a party that night where G50 was performing. G50 is a local rap group whose most recent album, *Lord Forgive Us*, tells a string of stories about living in the wake of Pee, who was recently murdered. I pick up my niece, who is fourteen at the time, with the album blasting to prepare for their performance. She sits in the car and says, "Who this?"

I smile. Even her developing voice had learned how to make "who this" sound more like skepticism than inquiry. She tells me she likes the song. She wants to know *who this* to decide what type of like she would reserve for it. Music is relational.

We pull up to Walmart. Affordable groceries always come with a price. Cheap labor or cheap conversations with folks you could go years without talking to if you didn't come. I speed-walk my niece through the store. I'm not in a rush; it's just one of those days that I know what I came for. After we walk around the store for about ten minutes, I direct us to the exit while thinking to myself, "I will just order the stuff online; you can't find anything in this small town." As we get near the front, approaching the cash registers that let you check yourself out, my niece slows down and asks, "You not going to get anything?"

"Naw, they didn't have what I want," I say as I stop walking to pause with her.

"So you just walking out without anything? What if they think you steal-ing some?" she asks.

"Then they just think I'm stealing," I say as I move toward the sliding exit doors to end the conversation.

My chest hurt.

I understood the feeling that prompted her question. I knew what it felt like to perform a version of innocence. I did not know how to walk out the store casually so that my empty hands wouldn't be read as criminal. Even though Walmart has blood on their hands, mine are Black. I can't (un)color them. I wasn't even really concerned with convincing the cashier of my innocence, but I hoped that seeing my confident strides could convince my niece not to feel guilty the way white people have set out for her to. Every time that I have bought something just to have a receipt when I exited a store, it is possible my niece also spent what little money she had to salvage what little dignity is afforded Black girls in the South.

James Baldwin in *The Fire Next Time* states: "White people hold the power, which means that they are superior to blacks, and the world has innumerable ways of making this difference known and felt and feared. Long before the Negro child perceives this difference, and even longer before he understands it, he has begun to react to it, he has begun to be controlled by it."[26] In think-ing with Baldwin, my niece could feel the social significance of her brown skin, even if she had not yet come to fully understand what it meant to be a Black girl in the South. It didn't matter that she was college bound and sang in the choir, because Black girls are twice as likely to be incarcerated than white girls, are disproportionately suspended from school, and are more likely to have police contact than other girls.[27] My niece did not know these things objectively, but she felt them from her collective experience of Black girlhood. She knew the myriad of ways Black girls are positioned as culpable.[28] They are responsible not only for their actions but for how the world interprets them. There are no structural remedies to the violence of knowing one's place in society. To know it in your flesh that you are a problem.

Charles Cooley suggests that we use the eyes of others to understand the meaning of our behavior.[29] For my niece and other Black girls, the notion of "looking-glass self" is a carceral experience. There is a fine line between seeing Black children and surveilling them. She felt the difference. It's no accident that W. E. B. Du Bois described those moments when Black folks see themselves from the eyes of white folk as a peculiar sensation.[30] Our insides blister when people watch our dance but don't understand our rhythm. We feel some type of way. What my niece feels is the carceral state.

We experience the criminal legal system beyond those moments where we take the dip out our back and hold the steering wheel with two hands because a cop car is beside us. It goes beyond using calendars as our way to tell time because clocks make it feel like our uncle will never get out. Ruth Wilson Gilmore says that prisons aren't simply buildings but a set of relationships.[31] The assumptions that make prisons so vital are the same ones we use to build the South. The logic that organizes prisons is that we need to surveil, police, and trap those we can define as other. We have organized the South around these assumptions, which is why Black mamas on Section 8 must get their homes inspected and walking into a Black school is like going through TSA without the promise of making it anywhere. My niece could sense that she could be safe only if the South felt safe from her.

Vibe is a commentary on how Black people as a collective are making sense of a wide range of racialized feelings and sensations, and points to the ways these feelings pull people closer to those who are racialized similarly. Black people are made to be out of place. A myriad of emotions make up Black lifeworlds, and being made to feel criminal is an important way our bodies know where we are. We feel a lot more than this, though. We smile in the face of pain. We laugh at absurdity. We love, until we don't. Focusing on felt criminality does not negate the way Black people can feel beyond what America has done to them. It does allow for me to sit with one way emotion helps Black people in the 252 understand the landscape of the South in ways that anti-Black structures do not provide a readily available language for.

There is this secretive place. Under the garments with brands and logos that hide one's precarity. Under the scars that show only the trauma our skin was able to process and solidify. A place even beneath the flesh, where we hold feelings and memories that if spoken over the noise of every day, something will break. Hip-hop is my entry point into this space. This space allows us to ask different questions and demands a different reading of the rural Black South. From Regina Bradley giving us on a ride in the Southernplayalistica-dillac to take us to the moment where she lost her father to show that trap music is a space of grieving to B. Brian Foster showing how Black folks have lived and taken pride in the blues but don't have to be the blues anymore.[32] We see that Black sound in the South is a space to work through what often seem like irreconcilable feelings in a region where Black people historically could lose their lives for feeling anything. Southern hip-hop's power isn't in resolving a crisis but in its ability to intensify it. Through demanding us to feel the hi-hats, 808s, and don't-give-a-fuck cadence to make sense of the music, southern hip-hop allows us to explore pain and ambivalence when those feelings have been foreclosed to Black people. The music allows the

Black community to further develop a capacity to use emotion as a mode of knowing. If southern hip-hop is where many of us learned to grieve and learned the honesty of inconsistency, then it is an integral space where we grapple with the complexity of bridging the emotional and epistemological.

WHERE THE SOUTH AT?

The sound of mosquitoes is drowning out the low waves of the river. Kiera and I sit on the top of a picnic table while we watch small waves hug rocks in the Roanoke River. Having grown up five minutes away from here, I can't remember a time when any Black people got in the water. Not even on a boat. I do remember reading a Toni Morrison quote where she said that water has a perfect memory. Maybe we were afraid to get in because of what we might find. Stories of our pain. Maybe we were afraid of what we might not find—ourselves. Too many times on the soil we didn't feel at home here; it would be difficult to handle that feeling from the water too.

Kiera was visiting the 252 for the holidays. She has spent her twenty-eight years of life in the South, with being born and raised in Halifax prior to moving to Winston-Salem. Halifax is the county seat of Halifax County and is considered the "white" town of the county. You can drive between towns in the county in matter of five minutes, without going through a stoplight, depending which road you take. Black people make up well over half of the county but rarely venture over to Kiera's town.

"It's just the atmosphere, and you can tell when you are not welcomed," Kiera says as she explains why she intuitively wanted to meet up here at the river in Weldon instead of in her town. "You know Halifax actually has a town part, and it be events there all the time. I never went, because you just knew we wasn't wanted."

The only few times I went to Halifax was when my mama was paying the water bill late, and she needed to drop it off rather than mail it in. Emotional distance can make a place feel far away and out of reach regardless of how close to it you are physically. Kiera's voice, like the park, is empty and still. She is narrating with a matter-of-fact cadence why Black people who live five minutes away from a town would never find themselves crossing borders. She sounds as if she's saying it to fill up the empty space in the park, as if that information is too obvious to be considered research.

Sitting with my eyes alternating between her and the water, I often interject softly with lazy head nods and "yeah." Conversations are like dances, and I want to let her know that I am following, and comfortable with her leading.

"I remember being a teenager and police officers smiling at us like they own the town," she says with her eyes down and her head shaking slowly from left to right.

Poor Confederate-flag-carrying white people have been painted as the image of racism in the rural South, but racial tension is often built within its geography. Some places don't feel like they belong to Black people, even absent racist symbols. It is known through the ways some grow to feel that they own the dirt below their feet, while others have had to produce alternative cartographies of the American South to find their place.

Kiera's notion of "it's just the atmosphere" points to ways the felt experience can serve as a window into the structural organization of space. Carcerality can be detected not only through the logics and technologies that organize geography but through the ways Black people emotionally register spaces as sites of surveillance, policing, and violence. Kiera and my niece both speak to this.

Due to its historical and contemporary affective relationship to Black people, the South has been experienced as a carceral site. In one way when I point to the South, I am literally referencing the states in which Black people endured chattel slavery and Jim Crow racism, as the 252 carries the spatial legacy of these institutions. However, "South" also holds discursive power in the cultural vocabulary of Americans. On occasion I have argued with others that North Carolina is part of the South, and more often others have pushed my thinking to include places such as DC and Maryland as South. In these exchanges folks have not, nor have I, pulled out maps to support our claims, but rather we mention slavery, Confederate flags, and other tools white people have used to feed their quest of finding meaning on a land not theirs. In this way the South is a set of assumptions about ways of being that extends beyond mere geography.

The 252 isn't *the* South, it is *a* South. It pushes, stretches, and often constrains our imagining of where the South is. This is also a story about the rural South. The area code sits at the upper peak of the Black Belt. The US Census Bureau classifies this area as the rural South, but most folks here, myself included, don't read those reports. We know we are in the rural Black South, because we have had to protest hazardous waste landfills. We know we are rural in the mornings when we smell the stench of the paper mill while we wait for the school bus. We know we are rural, because we walked to dollar stores after school and not a rec center. We know it because we pass farmland but don't know anybody making money off farming. The community knows the 252 is the Black rural South because rural Black people are erased from the US imagination of who is valuable, and we feel and live with that erasure. Rural South is just as much a justification as it is a descriptor. It has been used to justify various forms of policing, theft, and violence that have been enacted in the area.

To name the South, particularly the rural spaces, as a carceral site is a way of suggesting that the world-making and world-breaking ideologies of the antebellum South have had temporal and spatial continuity. The supposed Old South shows up and haunts various geographies that were made possible by American slavery. Marcus Hunter and Zandria Robinson named the southern Black experience in a very southern way when they suggested that Black Americans exist across various versions of the South with distinct anti-Black structures that shape the experience of place.[33] This is polite and inclusive, while also creating boundaries. To know where the South is, you must be inclusive. Malcolm X had a fluid conception of the South when he said, "As long as you South of the Canadian border, you South."[34] Malcolm X is not denying that an American South exists but engaging the way southern Black people and Black people who are beyond the region's colonial cartography experience the South not merely through geography but through the ways the racial logics of the Old South show up in contemporary practices across the country. This forces us to grapple with how the South made a United States possible and the ways historical racial domination practices of the antebellum South have been reworked and reproduced in the North, West, Midwest, and contemporary South to maintain a possibility of a future America.

Even through meticulous investigations, ethnographers have a history of othering things, beings, and places they have named Black. Rather than attempt to offer a grand theorization of the South or definitive truths about what and who the South is, I work with what Zenzele Isoke calls the "unwanted debris" of Black life in the rural South to create space to think both intimately and empirically about the South and beyond.[35] Grabbing at those pieces of Black life that are made out not to hold value. Those things we know because we forgot to forget them. Like the knot in your chest that time when you were a child and an officer asked, "Do you have parents?" as if "where" was lost from his vocabulary. I gather the often-unsayable pieces of Black interiority of 252 community members to hold a conversation on the varied instantiations of the South. The South is not a monolith; even within the 252, there are real regional differences. Using the South as a unit of analysis is an attempt to reconcile how Black people across the multiple Souths—watched Alton Sterling get tasered, slammed to the ground, and subsequently murdered while being held down—collectively *felt* something. Then watched how the criminal legal system was not moved enough to file charges against the officers.

While the 252 is the geographical space I labor in, I pull in examples, songs, and moments from across the South to complement and complicate what and where the South is. I do not intend to gloss over the variances and boundaries between southern places but take seriously Zandria Robinson's contention in *This Ain't Chicago* that southern cities have rich differences but also share regional, topographical, demographic, and social history that produces similarities.[36] The "carceral South" names the South as a space structured around policing and surveilling Black people in ways that movement can't escape. Since Blackness in the South and beyond is criminalized, carceral South is a frame to view the ways spaces must respond to this culpability. Moving through or out of the South changes the texture of this experience but does not change the national social codes written into dark skin. Our insides and flesh feel these codes and tell us things about place that maps and borders can't.

Since the carceral South represents a legally amended version of the antebellum South, getting to the rhythm of the South requires a step in the direction of Christina Sharpe and away from "political and legal answers to the issue of Black subjugation," to focus on the ways Black performative culture has allowed southern Black people to better name and survive their condition.[37] Thinking, working, and feeling at the intersections of southern hip-hop and carcerality from a rural context decouples modern experiences of Blackness from the urban landscape to think more fully about the expansion of the carceral state and Black peoples attempts at something that feels like freedom. Leaning on the intimate and personal pushes back against abstraction to work through the biographical and autobiographical to name how social orderings matter even for one's own coming to being.[38] This type of cartography locates the South somewhere down over there near where they keep the pain, love, and memories. I felt it.

RICH OFF PAIN

There is something about porches, living room sofas, and late-night studio sessions that if you are there long enough, they make you share parts of your insides with others that you hadn't really shared with yourself. I am a relatively progressive cis Black man, with a friend group that doesn't shy away from conversations about love, desire, and vulnerability, but being asked to help make and critique a person's art pulled me close to men's and women's softest selves in ways that often made me uncomfortable. Not in a bad way. The songs artists in the 252 create are often filled with secret feelings and memories that are unknown even to the artist until they put them in a song. Writing is a form of remembering. I was tasked to help style or make sense of these secrets. We remake ourselves through our imaginations, and I was being asked to dream with them.

Streetz, an artist I spend a lot of time with emotionally, and I meet up by coincidence at an album release party for an up-and-coming rap group on a Saturday night. I walk into a dark club that is dimly lit only at moments of the passing red strobe light. It looks like dark bodies two-stepping inside a lunar eclipse. As the light slowly slides across the room, you get a glimpse of the touching, rubbing, and grinding that happens only in the shadows of buildings where music and alcohol allow Black people to feel a version of free. During the day this is a restaurant that serves rockfish. At night men's cologne that smells the same way they hug women on the dance floor, sweet yet strong, drowns out the scent from earlier in the day.

As I walk through the door, Streetz throws his long slender brown arm in the air to flag me down. "How you feeling tonight?" he asks as he leans toward the side of my head so he won't have to yell over the DJ.

"Chilling, 'bout to get a drink if you want one," I respond as I'm motioning toward the bar. The bar is small with no drink menu. You just order what you want, and if the bartender can make it, then it's available. As he takes a sip of his beer, Streetz gives me his condolences for the recent passing of my mother. Streetz was also raised by a single mother. As a thirty-year-old father dedicated to making something that feels like family possible for his children, he is sensitive to me having to rethink what family means in the wake of my mother. As we discuss our mamas' legacies, Streetz reflects on how music allowed him and his mom to connect.

"Even though there is guns and drugs in the song, it go deeper than that, it's pain in it too," Streetz tells.

In our first meeting, three years before tonight, Streetz talked about how he watched his mother cry as she listened to his music for the first time. It was one of the first moments she saw him vulnerable. She listened beyond the guns and hustling and heard her son.

While trap music's contextual structure is organized around narratives of drug distribution and violence, Streetz points to the ways there is something more sociologically and texturally extensive in the sound. The 808s give Streetz's music a dark vibe, where you literally feel trapped within the sonic contours of the music. Streetz and other 252 artists work within the trap template to allow their mothers, and anyone else who will listen, to experience and feel a piece of the wreckage that lives within them. They call this pain music.

Underneath the 808s that pound the chest like palpitations and voices that have cried out for salvation so many times that even autotune can't fully mask the wear and tear on the vocal cords, are fragments of memories, desires, and hopes that if pieced together show one's vulnerability. We must listen right to get to this. When my mother passed, I had southern trap rapper Rod Wave on repeat. His cracked voice over soft drums narrating running with streets with his strap made room for me to work through feeling abandoned and having to find protection in myself. As a subgenre of trap music, pain music uses the sonic structure of trap to reveal moments of emotional and physical violence to work through what has been broken within us.

I felt Kevin Quashie when he suggested that the preoccupation to see Blackness solely through a social public lens with no inner life is racist.[39] The carceral organization of the South would have us believe that those who trap, scam, and rob to survive have no commitment to the soft parts of their inner selves and people they are committed to.[40] Pain music flips this logic on its head by using the feelings of people whose humanity it is difficult for society to see as emotional guides to making sense of the South. What is a better source of honesty than pain? It forces you to pare down to the essence of every question.[41] It makes you feel the stakes of survival in your bones. It reduces us to our core. I think Streetz's mother understood this. She found a piece of her son within a musical tradition that is popularly understood as void of sentimental capacity.

The US loves hood music, though. Deep down most of the country feels trapped, and the knocking of southern hip-hop gives us the feeling of breaking free from whatever constrains us. The white imagination has put borders on the genre, reducing trap music to being just trendy, catchy, and violent. Some songs do good work because they are catchy and violent.

Yeah, well I'ma gat totin' pistol holdin'.

Just rap that line around Black folks, and you will see. Trap also transgresses these boundaries and is as an intellectual and emotional space where southern Black people work through knowing the South. This makes the sound more dangerous than entertaining. In this shift we see that anger, rage, and hustling don't come from emotional deprivation but rather from a keen understanding of how the South functions. Trap is the music of the fugitive. It allows Black people to escape the ways the US says they should know and feel. It does what Richard Iton says Black popular culture does in that it provides avenues for Black people to construct their world with logics beyond those of dominant society.[42] The fugitive power of Black popular culture is expressed when Iton says:

The inclination in formal politics toward the quantifiable and the bordered, the structured, ordered, policeable, and disciplined is in fundamental tension with popular culture's willingness to embrace disturbance, to engage the apparently mad and maddening, to sustain often slippery frameworks of intention that act subliminally if not explicitly, on distinct and overlapping cognitive registers, and to acknowledge meaning in those spaces where speechlessness is the common currency.[43]

Iton points to the instances popular culture allows for ways of knowing and not knowing that go beyond formalized epistemological frameworks. It frees us from surface-level valuations and creates space to understand the political importance of disturbance and rupture. The vibe of it. Popular culture, hip-hop more specifically, makes us feel some type of way. Within that feeling, which is oftentimes unquantifiable and unsayable, is something honest about the place we live. For Streetz, that honesty is pain.

Streetz consciously articulated pain music as a type of subgenre that he labored in. Others bound themselves to the intimacies of this aesthetic even when they were not trying to find themselves there. I felt this with Paso.

"I'm tired of typing 'fly high Pee,' I wish could have died with my brother / I got all these questions for my bro, like why you didn't die with our brother."

Even without hearing Paso rap this over a dark gritty beat while harmonizing every time he says "brother," we can still catch the pain in these lyrics. This line comes from the last song on Paso's album *Emotion Pain*, where he is dealing with the hurt of losing his brother prematurely.[44] Death doesn't just change our relationship with the deceased; we are forced to redraw relationships with those that survive them. We question whether we could have cared for them differently. We are forced to fill in the moments left empty by their absence.

Pee was murdered a few months before I got back to the 252 for this project. When I arrived the area code was bound together by attempts at loving his memories so they wouldn't leave. Artists made songs to mourn him and shouted him out in ones that were not explicitly about him. DJs often played these records at local clubs. While I did not know Pee personally, I did know that Black boys like Pee and myself died prematurely in the South. As I listened to albums dedicated to Pee, I mourned our imagined relationship but more importantly him. I felt him through the music. I struggle to write about Pee because I did not know him personally. I do know that his absence impacted me in ways that other people's presence didn't. I do care for him in a way that is honest and attentive, or what John Jackson Jr. calls "sincerity."[45] Listening to video clips of him and hearing how his southern cadence carried vowels the way I do whenever I'm back in the 252 for longer than a few days, made me feel closer to him. I vibed with the 252 community as we grieved Pee collectively. It would have felt dishonest not to love on him with them.

In this way vibe signals how sounds and styles perform different emotions.[46] Pain music through naming and producing emotional realties in the southern context creates group boundaries and forges connections across space through the ways these realities signify to others emotionally. *If you can't feel my pain. Well, this ain't for you anyways.*[47] I experienced pain over someone I never met. I felt for Pee and our community because the sounds, styles, and rituals of remedy used to remember his life are the same ones that I use to survive. Pee and I were close in ways that maps and memories don't always recognize.

Tennille Nicole Allen and Antonia Randolph's work on the interiority of hip-hop and R&B centers 252 artist Rapsody, and they suggest that her album *Laila's Wisdom* is a tribute to the emotional sustenance gained from home, specifically her grandmother.[48] This is why Black mamas and grandmas are central to telling a story about where the South is. They expand the region's capacity to feel. To view the work that emotions do in hip-hop is to stand on our tiptoes and peek into the window of Black life to see how Black people move and sound when they are trying to forge a possibility of home in a place made possible through their bending and being broken.[49] On this journey of hip-hop in the South when I point to what could, on the surface, be considered non-hip-hop stories, I am pointing to the ways the contemplations and systems of knowing within the Black cultural realm are the same logics used in other aspects of Black life.

Southern Black hip-hop has popularized the term "vibe," positioning it within the commonsense vocabulary of Black people in the South and beyond. Just like music, vibe is relational. It is the social climate when ideas, bodies, and memories come into contact. It is often when our vocabulary fails to accurately account for the movement of our insides. "Vibe" names the way feeling structures moments, space, and time even when there is no readily available term to approximate what the body knows.

This epistemological shift allows Black people to know themselves and spaces in ways not possible through institutional assumptions. Even in the mist of the ugliness of the South, Black people have been beautiful. Beauty is a method.[50] Beauty is felt. Black folks lift their knees and slide their feet so smooth you would think the beat was following their lead. This is not because the song sounds beautiful, but because feeling good comes with a new choreography. Vibe gets to this. Sounds, styles, and visuals build emotional realities. They make us feel a type of way, and our bodies develop rhythms that push the boundaries of how the South sounds. This is the vibe of Black life.

2 Chainz gets to this in his song *It's a Vibe*.[51] Each of the four verses in the song follows the pattern of repeating "That's a vibe (that's a vibe)." Each time 2 Chainz says "vibe," he uses different fluctuations of voice, and the cadence of his sound shifts, and "that's a vibe" hits the ear differently every time it is heard. There are also three other artists on the track who all repeat 2 Chainz's verse and style it with their own individual aesthetic. Rather than the song feeling repetitive, each instantiation of "that's a vibe" feels fresh. 2 Chainz starts off with a smooth gritty southern flow, with Ty Dolla $ign pulling up next with a melodic raspy tenor flow that sits at the intersection of R&B and hip-hop, and Trey Songz backs him with a sensual soul vibe. Jhene Aiko finishes the song by infusing the "that's a vibe" structure with a meditative groove to ease the track to completion. While each artist works through the same lyrical structure, the way they style their verse produces different affective possibilities, allowing the listener to think about different relationships, intentions, and feelings. This is an instantiation of the way southern hip-hop artists use Black aesthetic shifts to both name and structure vibe in ways that communicate a Black subjective positionality.

In the 252 artists work from the contextual structure of trap music, flowing about drugs and guns, but style the emotional texture of the sound to communicate the despair of southern rural Black life. Pain escapes the binary of good or bad emotions and is situated as part of the structural reality of Blackness; however, Blackness is not reducible to it. Pain is not an indictment of an individual's failure to deal with their struggles in self-affirming ways. It really isn't about the individual. It is an inadvertent critique of a region that refuses to break from its old ways. Pain is a collective response to the ongoing juridical and extralegal ways Black people are made to feel out of place in the space they call home. The elders in the community would always say a version of "If I had a dollar every time [insert a lie, broken promise, or a mishap] happened, I would be rich." Hurt is routine. It is a resource. Pain music uses those feelings of neglect, abandonment, and betrayal to style lyrics centered on hustling through any means necessary to make something materialize from their pain.

NOTES ON *VIBE*

When I began to write *Vibe*, I wanted to write a book that my community could see themselves in. I know many from my community will purchase the book and celebrate me via social media, but I also know that my community is not the main consumer of academic writing, the type that gets people tenure. No matter how much southern prose or clarifying of terms I do, I cannot make this genre into something that it is not. Which is fine. The ones that are close to me have access to these ideas and me in modes that are not behind a paywall. They demand a piece of me that I'm not sure I would write knowing that white people would see those words. This book is for my community but will largely be consumed by people without an emotional and material stake in it. For this reason, I want these words to get as close as possible to something that I am not ashamed of calling honest. This why I center vibe. Rather than obsessing over capturing and displaying, it asks us to pay attention to moments, sounds, and spaces that we feel but can't quite translate to outsiders with denotation and interpretation.

Sociology as a discipline has attempted to observe, quantify, and index its way to an understanding of Blackness, and it has rendered Black people illegible doing so. Surveillance is a methodology for many. As a sociologist I recognize that vibe as a mode of methodological inquiry doesn't relieve me of my disciplinary baggage but is an experiment to reconcile the incongruity between the study of Black social life and the disciplinary formation of sociology.[52] You do not need to study Black people to know the South. But you do need to know Black people to know the South. Getting close to southern Black performative and emotional experiences moves us closer to where the South is.

Shifting from attempts to quantify the Black experience to vibing with it allows us to ask different questions about Blackness and space. Sociologists have measured the significance of race through life-chance indicators such as incarceration rates and wealth disparities. But even when Black people dodge formal incarceration and gain economic success, race still matters. When we slip through the cracks, we may avoid prison, but the bruising and scars of sliding remain. Black success is not a reflection of a more inviting social order. Vibe moves us beyond the quantifiable experience to allow us to think through how closing racial gaps does not indicate structures becoming less anti-Black, because we still must account for emotional and ontological violence. It asks us not to look at the rates in which Black people outsmart the system and do better statistically but to take seriously that an important part of being equal requires new modes of being that allow everyone to live freer.

To vibe with and sit within the emotional fold of a song complicates our understanding of musical text centered on drugs and violence. Black songs are lifelike. The texts alone that make up Black life and Black music don't fully account for how they are experienced. Textually, Black southerners have legal claim to the South. We have birth certificates, driver licenses, and apartment leases. These speak to a form of belonging. But calling the South ours doesn't feel as honest as we hope. This is in part due to moments of uneasiness when a 4 × 4 truck with an American flag pulls up beside us at a stoplight or those times when a sales associate asks us if we need help and the question feels like an interrogation. Those moments, in the words of Zora Neale Hurston, "gave me something to feel about."[53] They show that placemaking is affective work. Similarly, the text that make up trap music is centered on guns and drugs, but it just isn't right to say that's what those songs are about. To find what's missing, sometimes we must close our eyes and feel for it.

THE CHAPTERS

Vibe is organized thematically and walks through the various ways emotions are foundational to Black southern life. Chapter 1, "Let Me Vibe," charts how both the softest and hardest parts of southern Black people can tell us some-thing about place. Maps are rigid in that they are centered on the quantifiable and boundaries. The inner lives of southern Black people are explored to redraw the lines of the South. The chapter argues that the South is a carceral space, where Black people can feel the weight of policing and surveillance throughout the region. Vibe, as an analytical term, is used to help make sense of this. It is a relational approach in which Black people come to understand the various ways they are pinioned by history and the continuous unfold-ing of anti-Blackness. There are multiple Souths. Black people across these Souths invite each other to *catch a vibe*—to feel in community with each other to better understand where the South is. The notion of carceral South points to the ways the violence of the *Old* South is lived and felt across the South and beyond today.

The South is a painful place. It is the sonic production of Black pain that challenges the dominant cartography of the region. Chapter 2, "Use My Tears to Motivate," offers an invitation into the insides of trap rappers who bring listeners to the violent moments of the South to make claims about how the region is organized. They use their pain, grief, and desires as conceptual sites to work through what the South has denied and stolen from Black people. In this way pain music is connected to the blues. Blues isn't really the music.

The music is what the creative pieces of our insides produce after living the blues. Pain music is what is produced after living within the carceral confines of the South. It is a way of making sense of the world.

The 252 sound is not a natural identifiable product, but a relational process. Just as we can hear and locate the blues because we have lived them, the 252 sound is just as much about how we listen as it is about what is being said. You must know where to listen to hear the 252 in the music. Pain music encompasses a 252 vibe, not through a shared sound but through the ways it sets forth alternative possibilities of knowing, feeling, living within the region. Pain is central to this process, but the music and lives of the people in the region are not reducible to pain.

A lot of people in the 252 that make beauty possible are hood, ratchet, and ghetto. They produce sounds and moments that make bodies feel like they have a place. Chapter 3, "Hanging out the Window with My Ratchet-Ass Friends," seeks to close the gap between ratchet and beautiful, between hood and feminist. Black women's lives are songlike. Trap music is structured in double-time. Black women live in double-time. Double-time isn't just about doing and being multiple things at once. It pushes back against the controlling images and stereotypes that flatten Black women's humanity to justify various forms of violence. Black women can be ratchet, ghetto, caring, soft, and hard all at once. We just need to be able to listen right to hear it clearly. A Black-women-centered epistemology renegotiates and reimagines mainstream understandings of unruliness and disruptiveness. Women who rap about guns, drugs, and scamming offer a feminist politic of surviving the day-to-day.

Black women in the 252 are pushing back against politics of respectability. Respectable feminism forces Black femme-identifying people to get as close as possible to womanhood, which is white, thin, cis, soft, and middle-class, to be deserving of protection. It leaves no room to be ratchet, hood, and angry. Propriety is not conducive to needs of poor rural Black women.

There is an assumption that women are more emotional than men. This chapter argues that men's emotions organize systems, which renders them invisible. Black men in the South have had to mask the softest pieces of their insides. Through looking at southern car culture, we see that Black men don't inherently care about the car itself but about the ways the culture allows them to touch something, and it can become beautiful. Black men desire to make bodies beautiful, but the rigidness of the South denies them this possibility. Sonically, it has been through learning how to sing beautifully, queering their voice, that Black men have found more sincere ways to perform masculinity. A tempered style of queer performativity has been used for cis Black men in the 252 to perform Black masculinity in humanizing ways. Something that feels like liberation will not be possible for Black men until there is a commitment to bodies that move and exist differently from theirs.

Black people have carved out spaces of home in the South, despite the many ways Black people have been erased from southern maps and histories. Chapter 4, "We Turned a Section 8 Apartment into a Condo," is a story about placemaking, and the ways Black people move beyond the boundaries of place altogether. Black people in the 252 have done this through pain music. It is the poetic and creative experience of being Black alongside other Black people that has forged a bond between Black people and the region. Black people change the vibe of the South. This is not to deny or be blind to the assaults on Black life but an investment in Black folks' ability to fracture geography and slip into pockets that feel like home.

In those moments, spaces, and creases geography has mattered. Not because of space, though. It is the beauty, sound, and ideologies created in place that connect Black people to a larger Black diasporic spatial imaginary. Making space for Black people in the South has often come from (re)sounding the South. By this I mean moments we create new or attend to the often-unheard frequencies of the region. This allows us to have different memories and bodily experiences in that space. We can feel it in a new way.

In the South, "Who yo people?" is a geographical question. It is about where do your commitments reside and where do you forge community. Being from an area is not about ownership over physical space, but rather about reciprocal relationships with the people and touchstones that make a place a place. It is about who creates the sounds of life in a region. To be of and from a place is about being invested in the relational processes that continuously revise where a place is at. Black folks in the 252 have worked to un/map the South. They have pushed back against the boundaries of exclusion and rigidness of the South by looking for the South in unquantifiable and unindexed moments and sounds.

The closing verse takes up the idea that stories don't just give us information but force us to engage with what we could never know. They ask us to think about a way forward within uncertainty. The importance of a moment is not defined by how much it gives us structured and quantifiable ways of understanding the world. It matters by what it does to our bodies. Rather than coming home to capture something, I came to feel something. If I can get the reader to hear, feel, or sense part of what it means to do Black life in the 252, then I have helped someone get closer to where the South is.

CHAPTER 1

Let Me Vibe

There is a lot of the South. So much so that there is no consensus on where it begins and ends. The 252 is in the northeastern region of North Carolina and sits at the peak of the Black Belt. Even when some have said that North Carolina isn't "really" the South, folks here knew they were southern. They never needed maps to confirm their southernness. They never rehearsed southern choreographies. They existed here and that was enough. The way they sit in history proved their southernness. The history of slavery and Jim Crow lingers in the dust over the region's large farms that still don't make Black people any money. The history is in the follow-through of our jump shots, because Black kids had to learn how to shoot in double rim hoops at the outside courts. Only people who lived in the white part of Halifax County were eligible to get a card at T. J. Davis Recreation Center and play indoors. The 252 is a South. This is a story about how we know where and what the South is through how we feel our Blackness in place. The way the softest parts of ourselves can tell us *something* about *somewhere*, when the rigidness of maps refuses to redraw their lines to accommodate new *somebodies*.

Sabrina, unaware of the ongoing Supreme Court case *Silver et al. vs. Halifax County Board of Commissioners*, centered on racial inequality and school funding, moves with her son Jon from the projects in Weldon to Roanoke Rapids. Weldon is a small town that is 74 percent Black, with a median household income of $37,000. It is composed primarily of trailer homes and housing projects that accommodate Black community members, and a Dollar General they grab items from when they are too tired to drive to the neighboring city.[1] Roanoke Rapids, only a three-minute drive from Weldon, is 57 percent white, with a median household income of $37,000 and has been transformed into a highway pit stop as the city sits at the half-way point between New York and Miami and has built a host of fastfood

restaurants and hotels to accommodate travelers.² This is the white part of
Halifax County, where you qualify for a recreation center card. The com-
merce of Halifax County occurs in Roanoke Rapids, resulting in more funding for Roanoke Rapids City schools, with the Black students in Weldon
experiencing contemporary de facto separate-but-equal.

The plaintiffs in *Silver et al. vs. Halifax County Board of Commissioners*
argue for the integration of the city schools in Halifax County so that the
segregated students in Weldon can have an educational experience compa-
rable to the white students' at Roanoke Rapids City schools. While the income
level of the community members in Roanoke Rapids is no better than in
Weldon, Sabrina's move was an attempt to evade the unequal dealings the
county reserved for Black residents.

"I had to get up out the projects," Sabrina tells me. We are both leaning
on her car that is parked in front of her rental home.

Sabrina's new home is in a majority-white, economically mixed neighborhood. Every home has its own yard, but the yards are still close enough that
you can hear the conversations being had on the neighboring porch if you
listen hard enough. While Sabrina's income status remained relatively stable
with the move, she believed that a more economically diverse neighborhood
would give her five-year-old son a space that felt more like home than the
projects did. A space to be a Black child. Because you can't really be a kid
in a place where the government sees everyone, adults included, as needing
to be supervised, managed, or saved. It's too much surveillance to be free.

Sabrina is looking at me while I'm looking past her neighbor's yard into
the next yard. I'm trying to make a memory.

"I just want to give my son better opportunities," she tells me. "Kids were
getting in trouble for bringing stuff home at his old school, since they don't
have enough for everybody."

There is desperation in her voice. The kids in school were fighting over
resources like the parents in the *Silver et al. vs. Halifax County Board of
Commissioners* case were fighting. There were punitive consequences if the
kids bridged the gap between school and home by taking pencils, crayons,
and other supplies out of the building.

In the case the plaintiffs were arguing that having three school districts—two with majority-Black enrollment and one with majority-white
enrollment—exacerbates funding inequalities in the relatively low-income
county.³ They want the majority-Black Weldon City Schools and Halifax
County Schools, which have a combined total of less than three thousand
students in grades PK–12, to integrate with Roanoke Rapids City Schools to
promote educational equity. Sabrina, unaware of the court case, like most of

the community, knew firsthand the dangers of a school system that would punish a child under the guise of fairness for bringing home learning materials. She knew the violence of it all. That Black kids learned more about obedience than the reasons why their school only had Black kids. They learned early that if they were going to survive with at least a little bit of their souls intact, they would have to break the rules. Moving to Roanoke Rapids was an attempt to get away from the spatial confines of the housing projects and underfunded Black schools to gain access to space and possibilities reserved for white folk. She wanted a geography of dignity. To live in a space that could hold her son, not trap him.

A month in, Sabrina has found routine and began experiencing a genre of what we may call home. Jon, five years old, has become socialized into the children's world in the neighborhood and generally goes into the next-door neighbor's yard to play basketball or to the yard of the neighbor across the street to jump on the community trampoline. The neighborhood ran like a community center for the kids, so Jon didn't need permission to hoop or jump. Some communities work this way if they see each other as a community. This neighborhood has a different flow of traffic than the Weldon projects. The projects have all the exits to the complex closed off except one, so everyone knew if you were coming or going. Here traffic moved freely because it was assumed that people had places to go.

One Friday, Jon's six-year-old cousin came over to spend the weekend. Sabrina let them go out to play. There is freedom in motion. Jon and his cousin shot hoops first. Both of their bodies not much bigger than the ball, they had to use all the power their legs could muster to be able to get the ball to the goal. Their bodies slid around their neighbor's front yard while a basketball with most of the grip peeled off slid off their hands as they tried to see who could outscore the other. It was tiring work. So, they took off their shirts and made swimming trunks out of their shorts. They headed to the neighbor's house directly behind Jon's home and got in the swimming pool. After a few minutes of their arms stroking the water pretending to swim while their feet hugged the bottom of the pool to keep their Black faces above water, the police came racing down the street. Moments later Sabrina opened her front door to a police officer and a dark-skinned child with a wet face. When pool water and tears combine, it all looks the same.

Looking directly at me while she recalls the story, Sabrina says, "Maybe they shouldn't have been in the pool," which sounded like an indictment of herself for allowing them to be out alone, and not one of her son and nephew. Moving from the projects to a diverse neighborhood was supposed to keep the cops at bay. She is trying to work through what went wrong. I lean my head, trying to look past her house to see the pool where it all went down, but quickly pull my attention back to her, because the weight of her voice lets me know she needed to be seen while heard.

"But they only kids," she says. "They are acting like my son is someone that needs to be dealt with, like he can't be talked to. I don't want him feeling that way."

I nod in silence. I can't get my words to work right so they could hold the weight of the conversation. I didn't know what to say that could hold any of this up so we could see the silver lining beneath the fact that in the projects all Black kids are the criminals, and in this economically diverse neighborhood, only her son is. Some things we can't run from. Sabrina began to see this. She didn't want Jon to. She didn't want him feeling some type of way. She didn't want him to know in his body, heart, and mind what the South had set on seeing him as.

For Jon, moving from the projects to the economically diverse neighborhood didn't allow him to escape being surveilled and dealt with as a problem but transitioned him from one mode of policing to another. This is carcerality. It is the many ways that the assumptions that make prisons possible extend beyond the criminal legal system and are used to organize the social fabric of everyday life. Policing and prisons assume that surveillance, punishment, and containment are the appropriate responses to social issues and transgressions. We take this logic and build schools, neighborhoods, and regions believing that we can punish and police our way into formation. Hence, why Ruth Gilmore Wilson suggests that prison is more than a place; it is a set of relationships.[4] It is not only how the state relates to us but how we relate to each other. It is the foreclosing of developing prosocial and loving ways of holding each other accountable, and rather investing in ways to discipline, expose, and dispose of each other when our bodies, desires, and behaviors don't live up to their full potential.

Black people often bear the brunt of living in a carceral state. The logics and technology of surveillance and policing developed as a response to the varied ways the South believed Blackness was inherently out of place.[5] That Black people, even before they were understood to be people, needed to be managed if they were going to be productive producers of profit and social beings during and postslavery. When the label of "slave" was destroyed and Black people legally became people, that transition, as Saidiya Hartman suggests, did not destroy the assumptions about Blackness that justified violence and inhumane treatment of them, but rather bestowing rights and freedoms on Black people enabled continued violence, as now they are deemed guilty for the conditions in which they find themselves.[6] The South's forced

commitment to the abolition of chattel slavery did not indicate a commitment to redrawing the South as a place where Black people could have the
softest and hardest parts of themselves matter to how the region imagined
itself moving forward.

I feel like this history isn't history. North Carolina is home to the first
slave patrol and subsequently the first police department in the South.[7] Jon
is caught in this story in ways that movement across space and time can't
undo. It is Blackness in the South that warrants control, and local systems
and spaces are always responding to that demand. Whether you are in the
projects or a diverse neighborhood, you are still in the South.

Jon's South is other Black children's South. Months after the police are
called on Jon, a fifteen-year-old Black teen in Summerville, South Carolina,
is assaulted and threatened to have the police called on them for swimming
in a community pool.[8] It's not that Black children don't want to learn to
swim, it's just that since Black folks were transported to the South, they have
had a complicated relationship to water. Weeks before Summerville a white
woman in California called the police on eight-year-old Jordan Austin for
selling water in front of her home without an official permit.[9] The South
must have left the South. What I mean by this is that a story about the South
is a story about America. The idea that Blackness is a disaster that needs to
be tamed, policed, and contained took root in the South, but it expanded
across the country alongside Black people when they migrated in search of
someplace to make feel like home. The ways Black people are disadvantaged
across the South and beyond changes texture depending on the locality, but
the violence persists all the same.

While Jon was having his idea of community confined to his 5,500 square
foot yard, in the *Silver et al. vs. Halifax County Supreme Court* case the plaintiffs have argued that the predominantly white school district has received
millions more in local funding from tax revenue than the two Black districts,
but the court ruled that the board of county commissioners is not required
to provide the opportunity for North Carolina children to receive a sound
basic education.[10] These small Black children walk through sewage with their
school shoes because toilets flood the hallway. You don't need literacy laws
when Jon and his peers have mold and rodents in the school and assigned
seats placed away from where pieces of the ceiling fall. Reading is still dangerous for Black children in the South. As Sabrina pointed out earlier, the
school became more punitive to regulate the school resource shortage, and
these dangerous conditions produced more rules to regulate the movement
and freedom of students within the school walls under the guise of safety
and protection. No individual bathroom breaks without a school official

ensuring the bathrooms are safe-ish. Limited movement in the classrooms
to avoid the dangerous spots where the ceiling cries. This is carceral. Surveillance and containment are the intuitive ways we handle Black social issues.

In 2020 when COVID-19 hit, it was rough on these underfunded Black
schools and all other institutions that served primarily Black people in the
South. In Halifax County 75 percent of people incarcerated are Black, while
Black folks are disproportionately incarcerated throughout North Carolina.[11]
The health and sanitation issues in Maury Correctional Center, the local
prison in the 252, were Black-school-like. The mold and lack of resources
are all there. This situation was exacerbated by the presence of COVID-19.
People housed there contend that the lack of sanitary resources and the
inhumane conditions produced more punitive processes within the prison,
with an incarcerated community member stating, "I'm supposed to be in
green clothes [like minimum security], but due to the virus, they're holding me here [in medium security]. I'll just let you know, it's rough in here.
We're on 24–7 lockdown. There are no masks on the inmates."[12] We knew
they would die. They knew they would die. Moments of unexpected crisis
reveal who we are and our obligations, because we lean on instincts. We have
no strategies of remedy to protect the lungs, dignity, and flesh of those we
are comfortable locking away. When COVID-19 hit we doubled down on
carceral techniques, even when those are the very processes that would lead
to death during a pandemic.

I mention Maury Correctional to show how schools are prisonlike and
prisons are school-like. They both harbor the unresolved contradictions of
the South. The South has always needed Black people but never had a place
for them. The South created Black people, but Black people had to be Black
people. This is what James Baldwin means when he says white people must
figure out why it was necessary to have a "nigger" in the first place.[13] White
people labored to build the South with ideas of Black inferiority and criminality, and it is the ones marked as Black who must carry this imposition into
every room they find themselves. When Sabrina said she didn't "want him to
feel that way," she was referring to not wanting her son to have to carry the
weight of the white imagination on him, to not know in his body and flesh
that regardless of where he goes, he is a threat. Our bodies are instruments
of data collection. They hold memories we forgot to forget and can detect
traces of the past even when it looks different. Our feelings know a specific
version of a place that plotting, charting, and quantification cannot get to.

THE EVIDENCE OF THINGS NOT SEEN

Around noon on a Thursday morning, I leave Halifax to drive to Wilson. The drive is filled with miles of highway until there isn't. I get off onto a long two-lane road that has traffic going in both directions. This road goes for miles passing only farmland and trees before you see a stoplight. Wilson is a small city in the 252, with its population sitting at the halfway point between a city the size of Roanoke Rapids and a major city the size of Charlotte. I park at the restaurant, located on a long strip that has shopping and dining options, and wait at the front door for Drop to arrive. He is short. But his presence fills rooms in ways that bodies can't. He is filled with more stories and life experiences than you would expect from a twenty-six-year-old.

We sit down and make small talk to fill the silence of the empty restaurant while we wait for menus. After food and drinks are ordered and we work through the initial tension of first meetups, I ask how his music is going.

"I approach it [music] the same way I deal with every day," he says. "We were struggling growing up, and you know in Black families on Saturday morning you wake up and your mom has you helping with cleaning the house. My mom would play Mary J. Hip-hop is my Saturday morning music now. It's my therapy."

I smile as I listen. Drop approaches music the way he does everything else because Black life is often songlike. There is a rhythm and feeling to even the most mundane moments. Our conversation was this way.

Bobbing his head to the beat of his song that is playing from his iPhone, he raps, "It's from the heart little nigga / I was ready from the start little nigga." As we are both leaning over the iPhone that is in the center of the table, I throw in some ad libs by repeating "little nigga" at the end of his lines. We carry on for a few and then lean back in our seats laughing at our performance. It felt good to be part of his song.

Telling him I like the song would have conveyed something about my musical preference. But joining him in the song and following his rhythm produced a cultural atmosphere that communicated not only my musical preference but my relationship to the song. Drop felt my appreciation of the song as he witnessed the way it changed the bounce in my hands and the way I carried my voice to meet him at the end of each line. Our bodily sensations and movements were telling us both something about that moment we had together. We were constructing the vibe of the moment.

Asking Drop about his music impelled the impromptu cypher because language often fails to approximate our understanding of and feeling toward cultural experiences. Defining and quantifying his sound would always leave something missing. For the same reason, I could not just tell Drop that I liked his song. If he would have not heard my voice crack as it searched for the right pitch to be in tandem with his, then that emotional resonance that makes social moments matter would have been unaccounted for. It was the way our bodies gestured toward each other so we could hear one another, our willingness to embrace my bad sound, and the laughter that drowned out the echo of that bad sound that told us who we were to each other in that moment.

Feeling Black life tells us something more intimate than any calculus of living. When I do push Drop to offer a calculation and definition of his music, he reverts to the notion of feeling.

"When I make music, some people will call it getting in my feelings, but I call it getting in a mode. My songs be about what I experience in everyday life, so the vibe is always different because I go through a lot of things," Drop says.

Feelings are a mode of making sense of cultural processes. For southern Black people, "getting in my feelings" is paring down to the essence of an experience by tracing the ways their inner selves were moved by an event, moment, or space. It is principled investigation into the way the social world unfolds in ways not easily quantifiable. It is sharing what was done to our insides when there may be no direct physical evidence of a happening.

Having performed together, the conversation feels safer. It moves from being only about music and dances around the softest parts of ourselves. We don't talk explicitly about them, but as the conversation moves close enough to our insides, we can tell they are instructing the choreography of our exchange. Drop begins to tell me about the clothing store he owns and how it is connected to his musical pursuits. His father owned a retail store that had closed. For Drop, this was an opportunity for his father to see a piece of himself in him, even when the other parts may have made it difficult.

"I want my store to be a cultural spot," he says. "Where local clothing brands can sell their items. Even if customers don't buy anything, they still get to experience the city, because we have the local artists' music playing in there." Drop's shop is across town from where we are eating. It is in downtown Wilson, which is understood to be part of the hood.

A serious tone grips his voice. Our lighthearted moment is gone. "It's beautiful down here, but everything looks so old. We got Black barbershops, beauty stores, Jamaican braiding shops, and really anything you want. The city just doesn't want to take the time to build this part up," Drop tells me. Drop is tethering on the rickety bridge that Black folks move on when they talk about their impoverished neighborhoods and the social issues that are there, without reproducing the white-centered idea that Black impoverished neighborhoods produce crime and disorder. For Drop, it is not Blackness or struggle that produces crime and lack of neighborhood investment. Black and poor community members are the ones working to make beauty possible. Rather it is government responses to Blackness and poverty that produce the conditions in which crime is possible.

Despite the prevailing narrative about the proverbial bad side of town, Drop still chooses to have his business there.

"We just all kinda know that the Black businesses are on the hood side of town and the white businesses are on the good side," Drop tells me. "We always felt that way, but we don't really know why it's that way. I didn't really know until I started going to city council meetings and connecting with folks. Then I found out about how they are redlining Wilson. If I would have applied for a loan to get my shop on the good side of the city, they would have turned me down because of the address on my application."

Black folks already knew about the spatial division in Wilson, but participating in formal politics in the city solidified this understanding for Drop. At moments Black people just collectively understand racialized experiences, even when they can't adequately recall how they came to know. They still attempt to make beauty, despite knowing that the structure of the South aims to undermine it. This is what Zandria Robinson means when she says, Black folks "not stud'n' 'em white folks."[14] Black people are informed by intergenerational collective memories of Old South racism, and rather than get worked up or be surprised at the racism they face day-to-day, they are often indifferent to white folks. They already know what it is. They recenter what and who will get attention from their inner selves.

These intergenerational memories influence what Drop and others have named vibe. Vibe organizes the emotional vocabulary of Black people in the South, from asking "you feel me?" at the end of sentences to saying "I feel some type of way" when an event occurs, and they are negotiating their understanding of it. While vibe is undertheorized, Faith Kurtyka has described it as emotional resonance, and Andrew Friedman has thought of it as a communicative tool used to transmit and perceive intuitive signals.[15] When we center southern rural Black people, vibe becomes a theoretical framework to view the ways in which emotions, even those we lack a language to approximate, help make sense of social reality. It is the aura and social climate produced when ideas, people, and spaces collide. It is the sensation that lets us know history is sitting in the room with us, even the pieces we were denied access to. Vibe describes the cultural atmosphere produced when people encounter spaces, things, and others.

Our bodies, flesh, and insides help us make sense of social reality, but the significance of these ways of knowing is often obscured by our limited emotional vocabulary.[16] Slang for Black Americans is rooted in the struggle to say, name, and gesture toward something honest about who Black people are, while being constrained by American language and ideologies that are not flexible enough to include Blackness in its conception of human. We have always had to get around the limitations of the English language. Vibe, in the way southern Black folks have contextualized it, is about the relational intimacies that Black people share as a group. Black Americans have never lost our voice. We just had to reach deep inside, past where voices get stuck. Down to our inner core to wrestle with how the most fragile parts of our insides tell us something about who Black people are and where they are at. "Feeling some type of way," "vibe," and "you feel me" are ways we have tried to verbally make sense of the ways Black people feel in community.

Rinaldo Walcott tells us that due to Black death being both a spectacle and disregarded, Black people die differently.[17] For instance, the rates at which Black people die from COVID-19 and police killings during the pandemic was spectacularized in the media, while the structural conditions that linked them and made both possible were disregarded. Due to Black emotions also being both a spectacle and disregarded, Black people feel differently. What I mean by this is that Black emotions are often exaggerated, in that crime and other nonnormative behavior are understood to be a result of Black people not being able to control their emotions, while on the other hand Black people are thought to be heartless and emotionless. When Black people do use their emotions as legit modes of knowing, they do so in a society that has no language and frameworks to understand Black feeling as having any inherent value.

Vibe takes us somewhere. It gets us close to understanding those inner registers of Black life that shift how we position ourselves toward space and people.[18] In conceptualizing vibe I am less concerned with defining what emotions are than I am in engaging them in the context of Black people's lives to examine what they allow us to do. Scholar and lawyer Janie Kim points out that an fMRI, through measuring blood flow, can detect whether a person experiences an emotion but does not tell us what kind of emotion or the significance of the experience.[19] It is through the way emotions take shape in the social world that we understand how they matter for the flesh that experiences them. Rather than engage with the psychological aspects of emotions, I am interested in the social implications of emotions, specifically the way they construct cultural moments and one's relationship to place.[20]

Emotions are inherently a social experience, and vibe makes space to engage the racialized nature of this experience. Black folks use emotions to make claims about the world around them. To be Black, rural, and southern demands using the most intimate capacities of your body to make a region that defines how safe it is by how unfree you are, feel like home. The way Black people carry and respond to the emotional weight of being Black in the South tells us about what, where, and who the South is. Looking at Black feeling is not a search for shared emotions among Black people but sitting with the softest and hardest parts of those who are socially defined as Black to understand the complexity of the South.

Black people be feeling. Since Black people be feeling, they be knowing. At least this is what my brother lets me know while we sit around telling parts of stories that our memory was able to hold on to, and improvising the pieces that may have been lost or that didn't age well. My brother never moved out of the 252. As we sit on our mother's couch and talk louder than the television, it feels like I never did either. There is something about my mother's couch and familiar conversations with my brother that makes my voice, personality, and body move to its old choreography. It feels like the gap between my younger and current self is closing.

Eli repeats the same stories from week to week. I usually react to them as if it is my first time hearing them. It is the pauses, facial expressions, and the random moments he chooses to raise his voice to a higher octave that make the stories worthwhile. Not necessarily the plot. So, there is always something new in these old stories.

"You remember that time they tried to get me by the movie theater, right?" he asks as a preface to a story he wants to retell.

"When the cops pulled you over?" I respond.

"Yeah. I already knew something was up. It wasn't even intuition or nothing, it's just the vibe is always off over there. I pulled over before he even cut his lights on, because I already knew," he says, shaking his head.

Eli tells me a story that I am already familiar with, and ironically the story itself relies on Eli feeling as if he had lived that moment prior to it happening. He uses vibe to invoke a sense of familiarity, or a keen understanding of what could and would happen in that moment. He distinguishes vibe from intuition, though. Intuition often assumes that the acquisition of knowledge or ways of reasoning occur outside of one's consciousness. Eli is linking vibe to historical patterns that structure ways of knowing and making sense of space. In Eli's telling of this incident, he feels both clever and defeated, due to his ability to anticipate being pulled over before being prompted to but lacking the ability to prevent the encounter. W. E. B. Du Bois's question "How does it feel to be a problem?" asks us to grapple with the felt experience of Blackness, and Eli's narration reveals how living as the problem leads to a perception or glimpse into the future, what Du Bois himself termed "second sight."[21] Vibe, like second sight, is not about Black people intuitively knowing

or being able to understand individual white people's intentions, but rather
it is how our senses can feel the way space is designed to function.

Vibe isn't about being able to predict racialized moments of injustice, but
rather it captures the way the possibility of violence is positioned within
Black flesh. Even if Eli wouldn't have been pulled over, the unsettledness he
felt in that moment matters for how he understands the South. The possibility
of violence leaves scars too. It is often the wounds that go unaccounted for
that blister and weigh the body down.

I felt anxious.

As I ride with Mike to Raleigh, an hour's drive from Halifax, to help him
run errands, I notice that he is taking a series of town roads rather than getting on the highway. Mike is a local resident who would keep me up to date
about shows, parties, and all events that you must know somebody to hear
about. Riding with Mike is always an adventure. We talk about sports and
life, but mostly we gossip. So, an hour's drive didn't ever feel like an hour.

"You don't want to get on the highway? It might be quicker," I ask.

"Naw, that's where cops be. I like to take the back way when I'm going up
here," he responds. As I have no real plans that day, I don't mind the extra
twenty minutes the back way adds to the drive. In the rural South we spend
a lot of time in cars anyways, because there is no public transportation,
and everything is distanced from everything.[22] There is not a lot of street
hustling on corners. But the hustle here looks like car mechanics turning
their front yards into workspace and lining the street with cars waiting for
repair. Because of all of this, traffic stops are some of the most common
instances of face-to-face encounters between police officers and citizens in
the rural South.

I ask Mike if his registration is up to date and he looks at me and says,
"You know it don't matter if it is or isn't." I am still not sure if his car was valid
to drive that day. I didn't press him to find out, because in a way Mike was
right that it didn't matter. Following all driving regulations doesn't completely
mitigate the feeling that police violence is always reserved for Black people.
The possibility is always there. Anti-Blackness is the vibe of the South.[23] Even
at moments that anti-Blackness is unseen, its energy distorts and disrupts
what is around it. It is difficult to quantify this. Mike and Eli could sense these
distortions. The possibility of their capture weighed them down, and they
found no recourse in having a legal claim to movement in the South. They
developed mental Green Books to move across the South to contend with
a cultural climate centered on Black surveillance. These precise movements
are *the evidence of things not seen*.[24] Our bodies tell us, long before the data
is published, that the crisis is unresolved.

CATCH A VIBE

"Cuz, I'm about done with this shit, man. Man, police hot as hell. You know what I mean? I'm just trying to live right. Fuck this other shit. I'm just about to jump off in this rap game," Bill says in the opening dialogue to his song "Flair."[25]

Bill is playing the song from his iPhone while he sits on his long couch, and I'm on the love seat to his left. Bill's apartment is small, but big enough for him and his daughter he has sole custody of. Bill is a thirty-year-old short dark-skinned Black male whose coarse beard is always stretched by his constant smiling. Most of Bill's music works from the structural contours of trap music. Trap music is a subgenre of southern hip-hop, which in its Atlanta roots is centered on dealing drugs and guns, accompanied by triple-time subdivided hi-hats, heavy sub-bass, and layered kick drums.[26] Bill holds his phone close to me while I point my face to the floor so the phone can be directly to my ear. The song continues:

> Keep my gun while I'm dealing, got to watch me from these spirits,
> He going to try to take it, cuz I'm going to have to kill him,
> Lord I don't want to kill him, Lord I don't want to kill him,
> Coldhearted streets done took away my feelings

In "Flair" Bill depicts not only the physical violence that comes with par-ticipating in the trap life but also the emotional violence of it. The opening dialogue indicates that Bill wants to get out the streets, but throughout the song we see that living in a structural climate where drug dealing is one of the only viable means to earn a living wage comes with emotional bro-kering. Being forced into extralegal work, while living in a heavily policed neighborhood, required him to suppress his feelings not only for others he may do harm to but for himself. Struggle makes us do that: to momentarily relinquish our commitments to the softest parts of ourselves to engage in behavior that will make it possible for us to feed the people who make having a soft self possible. This means suppressing your fear of loneliness, prison, or death to have the courage to do what nobody who loves as hard as you would normally do.

"How do you feel about this song?" I ask Bill. I had learned that asking what a song is about and what the artist feels about the song are two different things. Some songs can be about nothing but still make us feel some type of way.

"I was trying to catch a vibe," Bill says. "When I went and got locked up, dudes were in there rapping. I wanted to tell my story because I was listening to everybody else, and they were talking about the same things I'm living and going through. I know others can relate to how I'm feeling."

In "Flair" Bill is trying to evoke an emotional experience and invite others into that moment with him, or what he calls "catch a vibe." In the South, Black people can catch feelings, catch the Holy Ghost, and catch a vibe. They all speak to when a sensuous experience encapsulates the body and brings our insides closer to people, spirits, and spaces. Bill was trying to grab hold of the feeling of living in deprivation, being under surveillance, and having a desire to live with a piece of dignity and perform it. Beyond how the lyrics read, Bill used the heavy cadence of 808 drums, trembles in his voice as they search for the right pitch, and a narrative that ultimately leads to someone being harmed to make the listener literally feel what it means to be trapped. It is in the manner that Bill performs and moves through his feelings, or what Amy Wilkins and Jennifer Pace call emotional style, that the song takes on meaning.[27] The song isn't inherently about violence or drugs. It is about the motivations, desires, and fears of someone who must wrestle their emotions into submission so that they can momentarily be willing to give up everything to gain some sort of economic stability. Bill is trying to produce a vibe.

"What inspires this type of music?" I ask.

"The problems I face, and everyone else too. The police. Those motherfuckers is number one. The shit crazy because they just regular people, though, you feel me? But they are a big part of our life. Think about this. Let's pretend I'm a killer, nobody around here is scared of me, but if they see the police, they scared. They [police] put so much fear in us, and they have it in our kids too. I was talking to my daughter one day. I was telling her, 'You know it's alright, all cops aren't bad.' She looked at me and was like, 'I can't tell.' I was like, damn."

For Bill, policing structures Black people's emotional worlds. He pushes back against the idea that it is community members who commit crime that makes neighborhoods feel unsafe, to suggest that it is the heaviness of who and what police officers represent that frightens even the most courageous parts of us. Bill's statement that Black people fear police officers more than a known killer came off as a joke. I laughed after he stated it. But he was trying to communicate a sensibility that many other 252 community members shared. That police existence, even when they are not present, fills Black people's bodies and hearts with horror. Living knowing there is an individual out there that could murder us and it wouldn't be considered murder. The way Blue Lives Matter feels like a threat. Even writing it felt like my hands were betraying me. This is a testament to Bill's point that police do damage to our insides. Even without firsthand experience with law enforcement,

Bill's daughter felt the vibe of policing's relationship with Black people. Bill's voice lost its laughter when he talked about his daughter not having faith in this system.

This is the vibe that Bill was trying to catch. He wanted to sonically capture the feeling of stomachs dropping when police officers are around, and hands cramping when they are forced to type police propaganda slogans. We know we are Black especially when police officers are around.[28] Part of being Black is feeling it. No hands up, no selling loose cigarettes, no playing with toy guns, no walking in the street, no sleeping in your own home. There is no type of empathy that can reproduce how heavy your skin feels when it can be your death sentence. Living in relation to this feeling with others is part of the racialized experience of Blackness. Feeling differently together.

Feeling the vibe of other incarcerated people's song is what drew Bill to hip-hop. He felt his life in their sound. He caught the vibe. Anthropologist Marc D. Perry has argued that hip-hop facilitates a process of making and moving of Black people to allow them to assemble concepts of Black-self in ways that challenge nationally bound racial framings.[29] Hip-hop can both connect Black folks and allow them to imagine themselves beyond the race-making institutions that organize the landscape in which they exist. While policing makes Black people feel a certain type of way, hip-hop allows Bill and others to work through that pain and feel something different between each other. The vibe that Bill's music holds is that of being trapped, but new affective possibilities are created between him and others who hold that same precarity. This is where Blackness becomes more than the violence that is done to it. This is the communal and worldmaking potential of Blackness that is produced when Black people find alternative modes of relation.

Stuart Hall contends that popular culture, as it is situated within racialized social structures, is a conceptual apparatus for the development of a Black diasporic identity.[30] In thinking through a Jamaican diasporic identity, Hall offers his analysis of Tony Sewell's book *Garvey's Children: The Legacy of Marcus Garvey*, suggesting that the story of Garvey's return to an African identity

went by the long route—through London and the United States. It "ends," not in Ethiopia but with Garvey's statue in front of the St Ann Parish Library in Jamaica: not with a traditional tribal chant but with the music of Burning Spear and Bob Marley's "Redemption Song."[31]

For Hall, Black diasporic people come to terms with their Blackness through the forms of dismemberment that shape the significance of Blackness in particular locales. If Hall is correct in his analysis of Garvey's journey to his African identity, then for Bill his return/arrival to a Black identity went by the long route—through the streets of Rocky Mount, North Carolina, to the Eastern Correction Center in Maury, North Carolina. It "ends" not in a return to the past but with Bill's family and Black community members having a welcome-back party for him on the southside of Rocky Mount: not with traditional African drums playing but with the music Bill created while he was away. Bill was swallowed whole by the carceral system, and it was hip-hop and his community that worked to make him legible. This forced him to think deeply about the core tenets of the Black diaspora: family, belonging, and community. It was through being treated Black by the carceral system that Bill could feel the disaster of his skin. It was through living in community with other Black people that he could feel that disaster bring about the possibility for something new.

Vibe is about those moments, glimpses, and small registers that our body captures even when it appears nothing has moved. We live in what Christina Sharpe refers to as the "wake of slavery," so the supposedly new South is a product of this disturbance.[32] Slavery undid the possibility for Black people to be people in the same way other people are people in the South. Even if we can't remember or are denied this full history, the vibe of the South reminds us of this story. The bodily sensations produced in response to the cultural atmosphere of the region tell us something that amendments can't. Black people were granted a version of legal citizenship. But white people are still trying to convince themselves and others that they deserve to be on land that's not theirs. They police and surveil the land the way people do when they are in possession of something they shouldn't be. Black people peep the vibes. We feel the weight of a history that is not yet history.

FEELING THE CARCERAL LANDSCAPE

In the 252 the long stretches of highway swallow cars in the distance. The dirt roads are long enough to swallow cars too, but dust clouds form in wake of cars to let you know that something has been there even if we can't see it. In the version of the South my mother grew up in, she rarely felt the highway's ability to carry you for miles without anything seemingly changing, because she did not travel often. Nor were there dust clouds that warned her that someone who loved her was coming to visit. She lived part of her childhood in Section 8 housing called South Rosemary Apartments. There is one entrance into the apartment complex. Brick one-story apartments line the sides of the street that widens at the end making a cul-de-sac. I drive slowly into South Rosemary looking at apartments that have lost their shine. I wonder if they smiled at my mother when she lived here thirty years ago, or if they always looked like they were designed to be shelter and not a home. I wonder if the road had always been this unfriendly. If when my mother roller-skated around the complex, her wheels fought this tough terrain or if the road was smoother back then.

The design of space tells us what it was built for. I wanted to believe that my mother lived in a place that felt like home. That the roughness of the neighborhood now is due to age and not design. Rashad Shabazz has documented how lifeless and restrictive architecture fix Black people spatially in housing projects in ways that feel like being fixed within prisons.[33] Both colorless. Both with signs at the entrance that feel like a warning rather than a name. The law watches both closely. Both have quiet spots where men whisper about things that if said too loudly could make their lives more unfree than what they already are. But my mother told me happy stories about growing up here. Maybe I couldn't see the happy because I didn't live and resist here. I grew up in the projects too, just not these projects. The air went down wrong when I swallowed it my first time here in South Rosemary. I hadn't yet learned how to breathe here.

I call Streetz as I park to let him know that I'm outside. All the apartments here look the same, and it is too dark to see the apartment numbers. He opens his front door and waves me over. I walk in and greet his girlfriend, who sits in the living room with us. The air goes down my throat better now that I am inside. This feels like a living room that I am familiar with. Where life happens despite what the world has designed for Black people on the outside. Streetz, a thirty-year-old father of two, is a tall, slender, light-skinned male with long dreads. He has the vibe of Bob Marley, in looks and the way both can carry words and sit them down beside other people's inner selves. They speak to your soul. Streetz thought deeply about the world. He was ideologically committed to the liberation of Black people. His praxis was mostly confined to working low-wage jobs where paychecks came slow. Both made a better future possible for his children. He often asked them questions during our conversation, and they would work through their shyness and answer. He smiled more when they were in the room.

"I been thinking about what it means when we say we are Black?" I ask. What is it that is connecting us?" Streetz had mentioned the way Black people live a few times, and I was trying to see how he thought about a question that I often grappled with.

"The struggle," he says. "All the obstacles we go through and how they are there to make us feel inferior, look at what's going on with the police." Streetz points to the TV and continues to say, "I was in here watching Kalief Browder, and I was tearing up. It takes a lot for me to cry. I get on my son about that, because the world doesn't allow young Black men to cry, they see it as weakness. I tell him it ain't nothing wrong with crying, we just can't be weak."

I sit within this ambiguity that Streetz is highlighting. For Streetz, the police undo Black people's insides, making them feel empty. He sees this happen with Kalief. He was a sixteen-year-old child, wrongfully arrested for allegedly stealing a backpack. He was sent to Rikers Island. He spent over a thousand days there waiting for trial as he refused to plead guilty for a crime he did not commit. After his release, he committed suicide after having sustained years of physical and psychological violence at Rikers. Streetz cried at this story but does not believe society should see men cry. He wants to teach his son that crying is healthy, but that there is danger to being seen as weak. Rashad Shabazz calls this a "postindustrial carceral masculinity."[34] This is because housing projects, disinvested neighborhoods, underfunded schools, and dangerous work environments do similar damage to the body as does prison. Black men and women have had to adopt forms of gender performance that center on toughness and the ability to survive violence. While Streetz is trying to reconcile appropriate displays of emotion, his softest self sheds tears for Kalief, while his hardest self wants to burn down the world for him. His body tells him they were connected. He in part comes to understand his relationship to Kalief through the way racialized emotions are transacted between individuals who have been shaped similarly by social relationships and history. This experience is mediated through the carceral reality in which he exists that has its own affective demands.

We sit with Kalief for a minute.

Then Streetz begins to tell me about when he was seventeen and made a series of choices that weren't really choices that led to his incarceration. He doesn't go into much detail, just enough for me to understand. His little ones are running around, and we don't want any information in the air that would undermine their father feeling like the warmest part of their favorite memories.

"It is all the same. Even if you not in prison, something is always on us," Streetz says.

I nod in agreement.

This is what Sabrina, Drop, and Bill were telling me in various ways. It didn't matter if they were in a diverse neighborhood, on the Black side of town, or in jail, their bodies always felt pinioned by history. Policed by the multiple ways Blackness is condemned. Streetz and others could feel the weight of surveillance and policing whether in a prison or not. A range of institutions were responding to Black people in the 252 as if they needed to be watched, policed, and contained. Something was always on the flesh. This is not to say that to be Black is the same as being in a prison, but rather thinking about how carceral logics and technologies expand beyond the prison itself.

The South by design is a carceral space. The carceral South points to the ways carceral logics and technologies are inscribed in the geography of the South because the structural positioning of Blackness demands it. In one way when I point to the South, I am literally referencing the states in which Black people endured chattel slavery and Jim Crow racism. In another sense I am thinking of the South in the ways Marcus Hunter and Zandria Robinson call upon us to view it as a frame to see the similarities across all Black communities.[35] They contend that "the geography of the Black American experience is best understood as existing within and across varying versions of the 'The South'—regional areas with distinct yet overlapping and similar patterns of racism."[36] In this way the South is just as much about what is done to people in the name of geography as it is about space.

In the US imagination, the South is the place where the country's historical racial ills took place and current racial ills are only due to backward people who can't let go of their Confederate flags. This simplistic misrepresentation of the South salvages the rest of the country. Racism is the thing of the past and held on to only by white folks too poor to move toward the future. Racism is transformed into a form of nostalgia for poor white bigots. In this misunderstanding of the South's choreography, the South becomes simultaneously the perpetuator of racism in the US and the redeemer. Slavery and Jim Crow were babies of the South. This is how the South brought racism to the US. Using the South as a scapegoat for structural racism that organizes the US allows the South to exonerate the rest of the country of any wrongdoing. The South is a frame in which we understand racism because it is a lens the US uses to understand who, what, and where racism can happen.

The 252 is not *the* South, but rather an instantiation of the South. It is one South that is connected to multiple Souths, even spaces that maps would not consider South. Naming the 252 the carceral South is a shorthand to think through the ways that movement across the region has not allowed Black people to escape the criminalization of Blackness. Our skin has not gotten *lighter* with travel. George Floyd moved from Texas and met Derek Chauvin in Minneapolis. The South is mobile. Carceral South is a critique of Western cartography. The lines that it draws are so rigid it disarms us from seeing how the Old South has moved across space and time. Since the story of the

South is the story of America, this is an indictment of America itself as a carceral space. The texture is based on locale, but what remains the same is that Blackness has always needed to be contained.

For Black folks in the 252 the vibe of the South is a carceral one. Attempts at better neighborhoods and economic opportunities have been met with various forms of resistance. Maybe movement can't get us out of the South. Moments when Black people in the area code have felt free have been less about mobility and more about feeling otherwise. They have used sound, beauty, and creativity to produce cultural moods and moments for which tongues don't get as tied when the word "free" is used to describe them. They change the vibe of spaces. Black people are a vibe.

CHAPTER 2

Use My Tears to Motivate

In early 2020 Anita Williams Wright and her son and daughter were guests at a Hampton Inn in Williamston. Williamston is a small town in the 252. A white woman employee suspected that the three were not actually guests and called the police on them. With Wright's children swimming, the two officers and the employee confronted Wright and demanded to see proof of her stay to make sure her children were not using the pool unauthorized. Wright showed them her room keycard and was immediately asked what her room number was.

"Why do I have to tell you what room I'm in?" Wright asked. "What did I do wrong?" Wright pushed back against the line of questioning that demanded her to perform innocence. The officer's face tightened up. He seemed agitated. Wright's stern voice was undermining a system that expected compliance from her.

Wright eventually signaled her children to get out of the pool, while saying to the officers, "You're degrading me like this in front of my kids." Their dark bodies, with drops of pool water shooting down their necks to their chests, walked to their mother with faces too shamed to make eye contact with the officers.

White women are structurally positioned as soft and needing protection, so calling the cops when inconvenienced by a Black woman does not disrupt the ways the carceral system functions but upholds it. You hear Wright on the video say multiple times, "They listening to her story, but not mine." Prevailing logics suggest that America is a structurally equal and colorblind society, so when Wright gets upset and questions her treatment as a Black woman, she is positioned as an emotional suspect. She is viewed as erratic and criminal for not simply complying with police.

If Black people just comply, then everything will work smoothly.

What is normal and smooth is the US is for Black people to make themselves small, so they don't seem dangerous. It is choosing to repair our inner dignity rather than losing our lives. It is wet children walking past officers staring directly at their mother, searching for directions on how they should move their bodies to make this situation end. When Wright staked a claim at dignity, the interaction escalated. Upon learning that she in fact did have a room at the hotel, the cops ran the plates on her car to see if her background checked out. She is/was not a criminal. She claimed emotional dignity that was not meant for her, and the cops searched for something to charge her with because of it.

While white people's emotions have been institutionalized through policy and education, Black people in the South have been circumscribed. Black people's emotions have no life and power when it comes to the institutional organization of the South, and Black people are literally murdered for expressing emotion. Wright survived her encounter. But something was broken, and I am trying to account for that.[1] The sounds, movements, and gestures that happened on the walk back to a room that you paid for but was told you did not deserve are the unheard pieces of the South. The nervous silence. The wet footsteps. The hurrying hand motions. Those moments matter but are rarely sat with. It is within these often-unindexed moments that we feel the gravity of an event.

During the encounter Wright fought back trembling in her speech to demand a piece of emotional justice for herself and children. She was fighting not just for her children's right to be in the pool but for them to be able to show up to that pool with whatever skin they wanted to wear that day. She did not shrink her cadence to sound passive and submissive to prove she was not a threat. She did not uncritically give her room information but rather demanded that the humanity of herself and children be respected. She was hurt. It was pain that added bass to the syllables her mouth conjured. Pain provides an avenue to perform and negotiate emotional subjectivity when respectable avenues have been foreclosed. This is the sound of Black life in the 252. It is the sonic production of pain that challenges the dominant cartography of the South.

I GOT PRAYING GRANDMOTHERS FOR NIGGAS WHO HATE

Driving down 95 south with rain beating on my windshield. It's not pouring but has a rhythm like the hi-hats in the songs I listen to on long car rides. I'm heading to Rocky Mount to see Bill. Rocky Mount is a small city with a population of about 53,000 but has a violent crime rate that is double the national average.[2] We call it Murder Mount. Few of us know people who have had a bullet tear through their flesh. Many more of us know people there who look at living and dying and don't see much difference. Both are burdens on their mothers. In Murder Mount we know that death usually isn't a singular event: it happens slowly. It starts with being deprived of necessities and typically comes after desperation.

I pull up in Bill's yard, and he comes to the porch waving his arm, saying, "You good. Come on." I wonder if he thought that I knew I was in Murder Mount.

"You from here, right?" I ask as I sit down on the loveseat.

"I ain't been stuck here, but this is where I'm at, though," Bill responds.

While smiling, as he always does, Bill was framing his presence in 252, specifically Rocky Mount, as one of choice, given the assumption that if someone had an option, no one would choose to stay in a rural place plagued with levels of crime similar to those of urban spaces. Like Bill, I feel tethered to the 252 despite the lack of structural resources. I am connected to the region through promises I made to people who I love for being alive. They choose to do their living here. Also, through my commitment to people I love who did not survive the South. They saw something in this region that I am in search for.

"What's it like here?" I ask.

Bill generally responds to questions with long narratives. Here is a snapshot of his response:

They say my neighborhood real bad, and I used to feel some type of way. You can't be afraid of your own people. But now I see why, because you could fall victim. But like my grandma house. My grandma use to clean up for the white folks her whole life, she was good to them. When the old white lady died, she gave her house to my grandma, because her family didn't like it because it was over this way (referring to where Bill lives now). Growing up, my grandma house use to get broken into because we were in the hood. My mom and all my aunts kept telling my grandma to move, but my grandma would always say "ain't nobody running me nowhere, you don't know how

much I put up with from them white people and you think I'm going
to let my own people run me away." Now I really see what she talking about, just because you here and those bad things happen to you
doesn't mean it was about you. You can be the little hope they need
if you stay there.

Bill's family history reflects a larger historical process that unfolded in
rural North Carolina. When Black people were migrating in masses out
of rural spaces in the South to the West, Northeast, and non-rural South,
researchers followed and studied the changing dynamics of those cities.
What they learned is that through government assistance white Americans
were able to move to suburbs and leave Black people, who were searching for
their freedom dream, in peril in the inner city.[3] Despite these trends, a large
number of Black people did not move from the rural South and existed in
unincorporated areas and rural towns with white majorities. In Rocky Mount
there was no inner city to leave Black people in, but rather white people en
masse just moved across town with no intention of looking back—in some
cases just giving away the homes in the parts of town that held no value.

Bill's grandma was committed to not leaving her neighborhood, let alone
the South. Thinking about all she and my grandma have been through in
the 252 made me question what being Black, rural, and southern demanded
of the core of my being. Bill's grandma's insides required her to have an
unrelenting love for her neighborhood and the people in it to withstand the
crime there. She was committed to not leaving but building in place. She did
not want to be moved to a "safer" neighborhood, but to make *her* neighborhood that which was safe. To be Black, rural, and southern has meant to
make life in the crevasses of the country. It is to mend what is fractured. For
Bill and me, our grandmothers served as "othermothers" for ourselves and
the community.[4] They raised not only us, but any kid in the neighborhood
that needed a meal or care. They set a foundation for imagining community.

Bill, who is a single father raised in the othermothering tradition, uses
family as a reference in his music-making process. He does this within sonic
contours of trap music. The heaviness and darkness of the sound constrain
the body, leaving only the chest vibrating from the kick drums. Author and
professor Jesse McCarthy says that "trap is the only music that sounds like
what living in contemporary America feels like."[5] It is the sound of broken
promises and unthought dreams. The heavy thumps from the tracks mimic
the feeling of beating your way through everything about the South that
constrains you. What better soundtrack for America than one about grieving? While trap is often heard as a genre about drug culture and hustling,

Regina Bradley locates trap's power in its ability to make legible the grief and grievances of southern Black men and women who feel unseen and unworthy elsewhere.[6] The heaviness of the trap sound represents the weight of having to build a region that you are denied any claim to. Then saying, "Fuck it, I'm going to make room for myself here anyway." That is what trap does to the soul.

"I want to be more positive, talk about less bullshit in my music," Bill tells me.

"What you been working on?" I ask.

"You will see," Bill says as the left part of his face pulls into a smile.

Months after we speak about his grandma and him talking about less bullshit, Bill released a track entitled "Grandma Glovez."[7] "Loading up them thirties with my grandma glovez / AK 47 I done fell in love / The streetz want that savage shit, what is us."

It was catchy.

Listening to it, I imagined young, well-dressed Black men, like ushers on Sunday morning, carrying guns using white church gloves to hide their fingerprints. I have heard stories about why southern Black church people wear white gloves, and they all had something to do with slavery. I haven't verified the accuracy of any of it. I just know that those gloves mean something to us.

I hit up Bill to see if this was him being on less bullshit. I found out that his grandma had passed away since the last time we talked.

He was crushed.

I hurt with him.

I felt like I added to that weight, because I didn't know how to make my words work right to ease the heaviness of it all. Bill was tasked with cleaning out the home that was gifted to his grandma. While cleaning up, he came across a pair of her white gloves.

"I came up with the song idea once I saw my grandma's gloves. She never let me touch them while she was alive," Bill tells me. I searched the cadence of his voice, looking for it to tell me how he was doing. He sounded low. But found comfort in talking about his grandma.

Bill uses his grandma's aesthetic to rupture the trap genre. He was engaging in the process that Tricia Rose has described as artists bending language to create alternative modes of understanding and living social roles and performance.[8] His grandma's legacy was colliding with the grittiness of trap music to produce something that supersedes both the genre and his grandma. The white gloves that southern Black women wear to church are grounded in the Black aesthetic tradition. For Bill's grandma's generation, it was dangerous to be a visible Black body taking up space in the public, so

Black worship services became a space to be aesthetically visible and assert beauty.[9] Bill's grandmother's emotional relationship to her gloves was based on their aesthetic performativity—they were the assertion of her subjectivity in the face of a society that only valued her labor.

Touching his grandma's white gloves for the first time solidified that she was gone. There is beauty and grief in the gloves. Bill uses the aesthetic value of his grandma's gloves to connect not only with her, but with the young 252 community who see their grandmas on Sunday wearing white gloves in church. "Grandma Glovez" takes on a 252 vibe through the ways it signals a defining feature of Black 252 life—the religious experiences gifted to the community by grandmothers.

Using his grandmother's gloves to keep his fingerprints off the gun he is loading works within the trap logic and points to the moments, real and imagined, where those who live in concerted poverty feel the vulnerability of their body and believe that a weapon is our only avenue to safety. There is more to this than violence. Folklorist Alan Dundes contends alongside the text you must think through the texture and context in which works take form.[10] For Dundes, texture is the specific phonemes and morphemes employed, or what I refer to as style; and context points us to the social situation.[11] The context of "Grandma Glovez" is that it came in the wake of his grandma's death. This song is released after he made a tribute song to honor the life and memory of his grandmother.[12] "Grandma Glovez" wasn't intended to be about his grandmother's legacy, but rather speaks to the ways she is continuously woven into his life and art. "Grandma Glovez"'s texture is shaped by a sped-up tempo and heavy-hitting drums. Something on your body must move while listening to it. The rasp in Bill's voice lingers after each line, carrying with it the pain that one's body would need to believe that a gun is their own viable option to survival.

"Grandma Glovez" is an instantiation of ways Black people's emotional subjectivity is used to construct hip-hop, particularly living in the wake of Black death. Even when a song's purpose is aimed at turning up, the text names and performs emotions that are grounded in Black subjectivity. Bill's grandma's love inspired the poetic contours of a song that some would write off as a drug or gun song. This is a song about the South, which means it is a song about America. This is a song about grief, which means it is a song about pain. Pain, because southern Black folks have so much of it, has been used to build worlds that can't be reduced to pain. We can't just listen to the song; we must catch its vibe and feel it.

I KNOW YOU HUNGRY FOR HOPE, BUT SHE IS DYING OF THIRST

Streetz is one of the dopest thinkers I know. The way he takes his understanding of politics and the hood and weaves both while his voice is usually breaking through clouds of weed smoke. He explains to me things that I'm already familiar with, but he colors it in a way where I see new possibilities. Academics would use terms like "organic intellectual" to describe him, but I think Streetz makes clear that street smarts is an important mode of making sense of things.[13] Streetz can talk about how rural white substance abuse is linked to the Black substance abuse in the 252 through rurality and class, but racialized policing has obscured the relationship. Next minute he is making jokes about his baby mama cheating and having sex with somebody else until her box braids fell out. At least I think he was joking.

Streetz dropped out of high school at sixteen. Uninspired by teachers who would not make a fuss if he dropped out, he did just that. He hustled to be productive with his time. He always valued education but also respected the material reality in which he lived. After a year away from school, he re-enrolled and graduated with his high school diploma. Next, he enrolled in the local community college, given college is the path that is preached to dope thinkers.

Shortly after enrolling, Streetz dropped out because he was convinced that an associate degree and two years of his life without full-time employment couldn't adequately arm him against the violence that comes with living in low-income areas. During the next few years, Streetz moved to the informal job market, having run-ins with law enforcement. I do not want to go into detail on these particulars because I do not want to sensationalize extralegal forms of employment or those moments when Black bodies and selves are at the will of those sanctioned to use violence on us. Rather than point us to moments of police terror, I want Streetz's narrative to point us to the impossibility of the Black experience or what Marc Lamont Hill calls the conundrum in which Black people must decide which way they will resist death today.[14] Sacrifice education for food. Increase chances of police contact or not be able to pay the light bill. These are the choices of one of the dopest thinkers I know.

At twenty-seven, now with two children, Streetz reenrolled into community college as his responsibilities demanded new choices of him. Upon enrolling he was on academic probation because of the way he dropped out years ago, and this came with financial constraints. He set up a meeting with the dean of the college, and I imagine in that meeting Streetz explained the sociology of his circumstances, pulling macrostructures from above and demonstrating how they weighed down on the minute choices we all make daily. Whatever was stated, he was able to get financial support for his classes that semester. He was good on tuition and fees. But he still had to pay for his own textbooks, which totaled over $600.

"If I had $600 to just spend, I wouldn't need to be in school in the first place," Streetz tells me as he explains why he dropped out of school this final time. Neither being a dope thinker nor having a hustling politic was enough to change the reality that his degree was structurally unobtainable.

We laugh and enjoy each other despite this.

As I sit in the living room of Streetz's two-bedroom apartment, his two children are moving about through the home, typically running between the kitchen and their room. Whenever making mention of the future, Streetz cuts his eyes to the direction of his children. Christina Sharpe teaches us that beauty is an attentiveness to a kind of performance that escapes violence—even something as small as being able to watch your children move about in the home you share together.[15] It was beautiful the way his neck turned to look in their direction, even when they were in the back room out of his eyes' reach. Streetz pays similar attention to his music. He attends to a kind of aesthetic and movement that escapes mainstream understanding of beauty and art.

"A lot of people tell me I make pain music," Streetz points out as he transitions from his experiences in the 252 to his music. "It is struggle music, because that's what we come from. A lot of people say this is a bad place, a lot of people feel trapped because it's a small town and there isn't much around here to keep your mind motivated."

Pain music isn't an internalization or reduction of Blackness to the ways white America has made Black people feel, but rather for Streetz and other artists it is a naming of what has been done to Black people—a description of the emotional weight of anti-Black spaces.

I sit attentively as I listen to Streetz talk through his understanding of his sound.

"Some folks hear the music and think it is gangsta, and others hear it and they feel me. When I'm talking about drugs or prison, I'm just giving you a message based on the things I been through."

Embodying a criminal persona in hip-hop is not new. It has been a method to hear stories from those pushed out of the mainstream, with Christopher Holmes Smith asserting that this "preoccupation with oppositional personae is actually a camouflaged means of negotiation, a cultural alchemy where apparent isolation is transformed into contingently employed, tactical maneuvers designed to foster inclusion with more mainstream social bodies."[16] Pain music works similarly. Pain is a powerful lens to understand the world. It makes us notice the details. It makes you locate the exact source of an occurrence. While in pain you pare down to the essence of an experience to understand exactly how to alleviate it. Pain music is an accounting of one's insides. It is going deep down into the core of oneself and sitting with all the baggage and emptiness that one body can store. It is revealing desires, fears, and frustrations that we are told should not live within us.

Bill and Streetz take the softest and hardest parts of themselves and articulate them in ways that signify to larger structural orderings. Bill wanted to do this with his grandma's gloves. Streetz uses his experiences of feeling trapped and his willingness to engage in illegal activity to support his family to signal emotions that exist within the wider public—a desire to protect and nurture family. While individuals may not have done time in prison for selling drugs, they can vibe with the sentiment of sacrifice for family. When Streetz says that some people may see it as gangsta and others may feel him, he points to the ways emotions are moved and signaled differently based on positionality. Those who have sat between choices that weren't really choices will understand the vibe. Without a cultural understanding or feeling, real or imagined, of literally or metaphorically being in a trap, these songs will do different types of affective work. Pain music does not try to bring emotions and experiences that have been otherized into the mainstream but rather proclaims that there is knowledge in what has been othered. Pain, and other negative emotions, tells us something acceptable ways of feeling can't.[17]

This is not new, though. This is a generational continuity of Black people in the South using the ugliest pieces of their experience to make sounds that both encapsulate that ugliness and make beauty feel possible. That's what the blues *does*. B. Brian Foster shows that for Black folks in the South, the blues is a method of sense-making.[18] The blues is not simply music but the pain in my grandma's back from a life of work, which makes her cook with a chair in front of the stove. It is Black kids walking through dew-covered grass on the way to school in the morning with Walmart bags on their shoes because they can't afford another pair if they get these dirty. The blues is what we live. It is not quite right to simply say that hip-hop and its subgenres simply come "after" the blues. Everything is blues, which is to say everything is Black folks trying to make sense of, survive, and subvert an impossible and deathly reality.[19] Pain music is the blues. This means that the bodily sensations and cultural knowledge of the blues make pain music possible.

Bound up within pain music is what Ta-Nehisi Coates calls "the struggle." In *Between the World and Me*, Coates affirms that the wisdom we get from our struggle has fashioned the way we walk and move through the world, because the struggle, in and of itself, has meaning.[20] This is not to romanticize the way Black people contend with structural violence but points to our ability to know and make meaning in spaces that are used to convince us that our subjectivity is meaningless.

The blues, struggle, and pain for southern Black people are not individual experiences. They deal with the collective state of our community. I often felt that Premo and I shared the same pain. We were both raised by single working moms. We both played school basketball because there was nothing else to do. We both wanted something more than what small, poor, rural towns could offer, and we both thought we could write our way to whatever that was. I wrote a book about Black people feeling in community. I said that we do it through music. Premo wrote a freestyle. He said, "If it's lit, then I'm lit with you / It's a 50% chance I'm getting killed with you / Clip loaded, feet planted because I'm here with you." His writing does a better job at showing and now simply telling.

Even without hearing the way his southern drawl wrestles his syllables into submission so that each line flows like the others, you can still catch the vibe of what he is articulating. He is narrating his willingness to share one's pain and struggle even if it costs him his life or forces him to take someone else's. To share someone's struggle is intimate. Just like the blues, pain music is a method of making sense of the world. Pain doesn't just tell us that something was done to us but demands a search for the source.

Premo and I hurt in similar ways. One Thursday, Premo and I are riding to the bar to chill, and we pass tobacco and peanut farms, as we always do. We see these so often that we stopped seeing them on rides. We pass them and look at them, but since they are so normal, we don't process that we are looking at them. As far as both of us know, both our great-great grandmothers were tethered to these fields at the closing moments of chattel slavery. We don't have any official records. Both our families have always been in this area, so we just assume that to be the case. There is no real reason to pay attention to those fields today. Black people don't make any money off that land.[21] Some things never change.

What we do talk about in the car ride is our mothers' experiences growing up here. Both our mothers had a life of factory and service work that was so time-consuming and physically draining that neither had the capacity to do much else. The other parts of their lives consisted of caring for their children. Our fathers made attempts at loving our mothers but eventually left looking for dreams that America promised men but the South denied to Black men. Our mothers stayed. They worked and took care of children. Premo and I, both childless, did to the women of the South what our fathers did to our mothers. We chased dreams. We avoided finding immediate avenues to provide material support to our mothers, hoping that our dreams would one day love us back by paying bills.

I went to college. Then graduate school. I delayed work, chasing the title "doctor." My mother died seven months after I got my PhD. Premo chased music. He hopes this race is worth the sacrifices.

"I started rapping at thirteen, and my mom would listen to my music. But I don't think she thought I would still be doing it this long. When I became an adult, it started causing problems when I was living with her. I would come home at late hours because I was in the studio. She was struggling, and it was hard for me to help because I was investing in my music. When I spent my last forty dollars on studio time, she kicked me out. But that's the past and it's part of the journey and I'm cool with it, you feel me?"

I don't verbally answer the question. I nod, while I sit with what was said.

I knew a piece of what he was feeling. Pursuing education is seen as a legit reason not to be in a financial position to provide for the one parent who took care of you. But bills don't know that. I knew that it hurt Premo to not be able to provide. His cadence said it. After Premo and others make compelling statements, they say, "You feel me?" This is more of a conjunction than a question. It invites the other person to share a piece of who they are to connect with the current mood. It is a way to find mutual ground and stand together even if it feels like both of you are drowning.

I do feel Premo. Due to his material conditions, creating music is also part of the struggle he aims to document. It makes sense that if your mother is struggling, to use the last bit of money you have for food and bills. I also know what it feels like to have an inner self. To desire a world shut off to you. To treat your desire and other emotions as rational ways of doing life. To feel someone is less about appropriating their emotions through sympathy or empathy than positioning their emotions as valid enough to warrant our attention in constructing our understanding of how they engage the world. Premo and others use their struggle not only to produce pain music, but to reflect upon society and come to understand the world in ways that don't neatly square with mainstream assumptions.

THIS WHAT IT SOUNDS LIKE WHEN THUGS CRY

Amp was murdered in 2020. I did not know Amp personally. I only knew his face. When I heard his name in conversation, I could trace out his round face in my memory. I always painted him wearing a fitted cap that had a sports team on it. We knew the same people but were always a grade or street away from each other. Amp was murdered a few blocks away from where Jon moved from in Weldon. Jon didn't have to hear the gunshots. When you hear gunshots in small rural Black towns, it is not a matter of if you know the victim but how connected to them you are. Everyone knows everybody here. Even if they don't talk, they will at least be able to draw up a face when they hear their name.

I met with Amp's cousin Mone, an artist from Weldon, a few weeks before Amp was murdered. He recently released an album, and I wanted to talk about what inspired it. The conversation was not about death, but the possibility of death weighed down our sentences. Mone's voice is deep and wide. Far down in the vastness of his speech you could hear that death was approaching. It always is.

"How has Weldon been?" I ask. I grew up in the projects that Jon lived in, which is a few blocks from where Amp will be murdered.

"There have been shootouts for three weeks straight. You know how it is in these small rough areas, the lifestyle is different," Mone responds. I do know what Mone means. In a small, rural, poor, primarily Black community, everyone is connected. When violence happens, the town is fractured. People choose which side of the crack they will stand on. The first instance of violence is usually structural. It's the lack of resources, jobs, teachers, rec centers, and everything else that makes space feel safe. Once violence is set in motion, it is hard to stop. We are a small, underserved community, and even when we fight, we know that we are the only ones who will mourn each other. I don't know why the person that murdered Amp did it. I do know they turned themselves in.

Mone had not known what would happen to Amp. He did know our hometown well enough to mention shootouts when I asked generally about home. Amp did not come up in our conversation. He knew what was coming, but he had not drawn Amp's round face and fitted cap on the scene.

The day following Amp's murder, Facebook was filled with Long Live Amp posts. My timeline was a string of stories, pictures, and videos that told pieces of Amp's life. He was kind and funny. Someone that I would have been close with if the grades and streets that separated us were not so wide. If poor Black neighborhoods weren't so heavily policed and under-resourced making Black people cling to specific spaces, maybe we could have run into each other. If the south wasn't a carceral space, maybe I would have crossed the street for Amp or him for me. Maybe our worlds would have been our world.

Following the day that Facebook was dedicated to Amp, Mone released a music video in honor of Amp's life. In forty-eight hours after Amp's murder,

Mone had written, recorded, and filmed a video to a song about Amp. The video had people wearing T-shirts that had Amp's face floating in clouds. Adults walked the street smoking Black and Milds and drinking alcohol directly out the bottle. Children danced and threw up hand signs with fingers so small that Amp would have to squint from the clouds to see what they were saying to him. It was produced so fast, as if the community was already prepared. Death comes so often; we have perfected our rituals of care. I hate that we are so good at mourning.

I pause. I search for my headphones to watch for the music video of Mone and LulZac's song "Bring Em All Back."[22] "Them niggas they can't come back / To the South, it ain't no more of that / Long live Amp thought you were coming back / My grandma pray on every homicide / When I'm out here it's time to ride." This is the chorus of the song. Working within the structural contours of trap music, this song signals a failure to protect a loved one, so now boundaries are going to be placed on who can move through their city, and they will be enforced with violence if need be. Listening to the song there is *something* particularly 252 about the sound. Sounds are social, local, and intimate.[23] This song feels 252. Musicologist Nina Eidsheim says if two voices rap or sing "the same pitch at the same dynamic and for the same duration, timbre is what allows us to distinguish between them."[24] Timbre, or that something-ness, is not an objective feature, but rather listeners define and agree upon what this is.

This song felt 252 in part because of how I listened to it. It was the affective world that was built into the trap structure that allowed me to sense the 252 in the sound. You can hear the way they say South like [souf], like most southern people. You could also hear more 252 specific pronunciations such as "strong" being pronounced [straw-on]. I hear the names of community members used as poetic devices. I can also hear what was not audible. Like the mosquitoes. Seeing everyone piled onto a street that I use to hang out on at night made me feel old prickly bites on the soft part of my arms. Behind the new clothes, alcohol, and beats I hear pain. Two young Black men harmonically rapping a eulogy while the community attempts to lip sync along to a song that was written a day ago. They only had a few hours to learn the song. A few more to learn what it meant to live without Amp.

Trap music generally has a tempo between 100–176 beats per minutes (BPM).[25] Within this tempo songs can sound both fast and slow. They are typically a combination of R&B and rap samples, so where you listen at in the song determines how you hear it. Some would consider the drums to be the most important piece of the trap structure. Simple hi-hats, snares, and an 808 on the one beat gives trap the ability to bend airwaves with its vibrations.[26] In the 252 that something-ness of a song is less about song structure, and more about the process of using 252 subjectivity to construct musical representations. This brings us back to the blues. Blues isn't really the music. The music is what the creative pieces of our insides produce after living the blues. The blues is heard and felt through the way Black southerners live and make sense of the world. I heard the 252 in "Bring Em All Back" through what I lived in the 252 and what was being lived in the video. That living is painful. In the video I heard and saw a search for a sign that Amp's life had meaning. That he didn't just live and die in a rural poor Black town. Hoping that space between his birth and death produced something. Because Amp's life had to matter.

"I don't really rap about anything special, just my personal life. My voice bleeds, so people can hear my pain," Mone tells me three weeks before Amp is murdered. I didn't really know what Mone meant by his voice bleeds. I made a memory of that statement, though. I do know how I felt when I made that memory. It felt like Mone was saying that you don't have to rap about anything special when you rap about what's honest. What's important is for people to feel the worry, despair, and anger. If they can catch that vibe, if they accept the invitation into the most tender parts of a hood nigga's insides, then they can hear him and where he comes from. The music is less about the guns and drugs that get waved around than about the emotional experiences imbued into that form.

On "Bring Em All Back," Mone slowed down the BPM to give the song a soul vibe. This slowed tempo allowed Mone to sing and harmonize at key moments on the track to direct our attention to what is emotionally significant. We see this in the second verse when LulZac raps, "Have you ever seen a thug cry / I look at Tina like my mama, that's my thug yeah (that's my lady) / Long live Meka, I know she cracking up with Bud now."

Lul Zac's voice sounds broken, as if it yelled out to God one too many times. It sounds as if he never had vocal training but had learned how to mourn so well that we can feel everything wrong about the South in his voice. This brokenness is what connects him to the 252.[27] In pain music it is not about how well you sing but about making the listener feel something. Even the most distressed voices can do that. These songs encompass a 252 vibe, not through a shared sound but through the ways in which the song produces an emotional experience that sets forth a 252 identity.

Voices are not natural to us.[28] We are not born sounding Black, poor, or rural. Those are boundaries placed on speech by listeners so they can better process what they are hearing. We do speak in community, though. We learn where to stress our voices and what tones set fire to the inner self of those we are around. Sound is a relational project where the speaker gauges a field of cultural possibilities and produces a sound hoping to be read in a particular way, while the listener, from their subjective standpoint, ascribes status characteristics to what is heard. The 252 sound is not a natural identifiable product but a relational process. A 252 sound is just as much about how we listen as it is about what is being said. To hear the 252 in "Bring Em All Back," I had to catch the vibe. I first had to know the 252 to be able to look for it. Pain is what I listened for.

PAIN MUSIC IN THE CARCERAL SOUTH

Being home and trying to write a book about it makes desires, stories, and commitments collide in my mind. When does a moment stop being research and become living? Maybe living is research. In moments where I wasn't consumed by grief, I attempted to understand Amp's death. I wanted to be able to tell my community something about the relationship between Amp's life and the world we live in to allow them not to hurt as much. When I thought about Amp's life, his memory kept crashing into the stories I heard from many young Black men and women in the South. These stories suggest that when the nature of the South is violent and not restricted to the South, there is often no such thing as good choices. That moving within and out of the South would provide no relief. Time doesn't heal old wounds. When what caused those wounds hasn't been addressed, old wounds do the most damage. Drop points to this one evening when we are at the bar reflecting on our young adult years. We discuss versions of ourselves and moments that don't neatly represent who we have grown to be.

"Don't get me wrong, I'm not saying I never took a gun to the club or did other wrong things," he says. "When I put those experiences in my music, people can listen and say, 'Oh he a thug. That's gangsta music.' If you think I'm gangsta, then that's just your opinion. I'm just telling you what I go through. I'm just telling you my struggle and what I will do to make sure my family straight."

This reminded me of Streetz. What was caught within the walls of that dark bar was Drop talking through moments of violence he engaged in that don't inherently speak to who he is. The violence, just like Blackness, becomes a spectacle. Drop and others link the text in their music centered on guns and drugs to the real and imagined realities of being Black in the carceral South and having limited options to keep one's body safe and to adequately secure material stability. When minimum wage comes too slowly, and bills don't come at all because they never leave, every moment is about survival. Survival has no schedule. At any moment our bodies and what little we have accumulated can be taken by someone else who is behind schedule on bills, on surviving. This is the feeling Drop is trying to produce when he talks about taking a gun to the club. For those who are desperate to eat and keep housing, any moment is a moment to secure some type of material relief. For Drop, that means every moment is a moment that we are all unsafe and need protection.

However, Drop also suggested that he and other Black community members can't let their structural reality become an excuse for engaging in unproductive behavior.

"If Black people already know the police are watching and that they target us, then we need to be proactive to make sure nothing wrong happens," Drop says as he looks directly at me. In this way Drop puts responsibility on Black people to pay attention to laws more tightly, since they already know that Black folks face disadvantage in the criminal legal system. This is where Drop's story connects with Amp's story. Drop and others understand the structure of the South disadvantages poor Black people. The institutions provide little to no redress for the pain of everyday life. It often requires extralegal forms of work and protection to survive the South. Drop and others also suggest that Black people know the risks of this lifestyle. That the very things we must do to survive are often what may be the death of us. Pain music is used to critique the systems that concentrate disadvantage onto poor Black people. It also wants us to feel the horror of having engaged in behavior that can lead to violence filling the environment.

The critiques in pain music are not as literal as ones in what people would call conscious rap. The structural critiques in pain music can be seen through what Christina Sharpe describes as "theorizing the multiple meanings of that abjection through inhabitation."[29] Pain music puts you at the center of the event. It forces you to feel the messiness of it all. It puts one's subjectivity on full display. It doesn't run from the terrible, vulnerable, and undesirable. It offers an alternative narrative of violence. A more honest one. What if Amp, I, or any one of us were behind the gun? Does the narrative change? Do we become the monster? Pain music doesn't reduce individuals to the moment of violence but seeks to understand the context that produced that moment. It aims to love on those who got to that moment through choices that weren't really choices. Mone produced a video to honor Amp despite what happened to bring him to that moment of violence.

"Bring Em All Back" had thousands of views on YouTube in the first day of its release. The video comes on with the screen frame and quality like the color TVs of the 1960s. The children from Amp's family and community are standing in the street of his hometown holding up Ls with both hands.[30] The video takes place on a single street with the camera shifting back and forth between community members—some with shirts and pants with Amp's name and face on them. The video also incorporates a behind-the-scenes videography style where at different moments in the video it flashes to footage from the vigil that was previously held to honor Amp the day after his death. While the video showcases around thirty community members, this video is a product of a larger community investment.[31] It took a community to make this video possible. To produce a track and video to honor Amp—that has footage from his vigil, clothing with his name and picture, and a good-sized gathering of people—immediately following his death required his community to put their worlds on hold for him. This is a level of care for Black death that challenges how state institutions position Black people.

The choices that brought Amp to the moment of being in front of the gun did not matter. The community needed no investigation to know if he was worthy of all our lives stopping. The South demands those moments of violence. We knew it was bigger than who was in front of and behind the gun. Mone knew this in our conversation three weeks before Amp's death.

"All these police around here and they don't really care about what's going on, or if this neighborhood feels safe," Mone says as if he is foreshadowing losing the life of a community member. Mone's neighborhood, through policing and the establishment of borders, is a prisonlike environment and is unsafe even with an abundance of police activity. Mone's observation sets forth one of the most striking similarities between prisons and poor Black neighborhoods: state surveillance does not produce safer spaces. It only produces a condition where death and police watch Black people alongside each other.[32] Even though Amp and others' deaths may not directly come from the barrel of a police gun, the state always bears witness to the conditions in which Black people live and chooses not to see these conditions as issues.

Mone and the community urgently cared for Amp because there would be no state-organized recognition. This urgency around archiving Amp's life is a form of care, which Sharpe cites as an epistemological intervention on how state institutions engage Black life.[33] Slavery and the carceral state not only are systems of racial hierarchy but shape how we understand who and what has a right to all the things that come with being alive. Feelings, desires, care. This means that the structure of the South determines who can be victims, whose suffering registers, and who/what has no capacity to suffer.[34] It doesn't matter if Amp lived a fast life or if the ways he coped with being Black, rural, and poor were not the healthiest—he deserved to be remembered. To make "Bring Em All Back" the 252 community stopped and collectively produced an archive that was a testament to the fact that Amp had once lived. Death could not change that. Both history and remembering are political. If we did not remember Amp, then there would be no need to remember the conditions that produced his death. The point of pain music is to look at the world and to be honest about it. It is difficult to tell an honest story about being poor and Black in the South without pain and death.

Pain music deals with the impossible choices of Black life in the South. It takes us to moments of violence to reveal something about the structure of the South. Mane, a member of the rap group G50 along with Mone, does this through a series of solo albums titled *Live from Hurley Ave* and several group albums with Mone. I lay back on my bed with my eyes closed and headphones pushing my ears into the side of my head, listening to Mane's albums hoping to find meaning in all this hurt. *Live from Hurley Ave 3* was largely about the death of Pee, who was murdered just before I moved back to the 252. This is the album I listened closely to with hopes of better understanding Amp.

On "June 17th," the final song on *Live from Hurley Ave 3*, Mane documents his final moments seeing his brother Pee.[35]

"Think about it," is what I should have said,
But he was trying to get that bag, so I couldn't say it,
And if I had to do it again, I wouldn't say it,
Then later Reek walked up in the crib, like "Pee Wee fucking dead."

Four years after his death, I have found only three news reports about this incident, with none of them being longer than ten sentences. Those reports contend that officers were responding to an unknown problem, and that no known motives existed, as if Pee wasn't facing poverty, underemployment, and navigating a carceral state like the other Black boys in the neighborhood. There is always a motive.

Pee's death was reduced to a couple of news articles that positioned his death as happenstance, as if dying prematurely is just what Black boys do. In documenting his last moments with Pee, Mane forces the listener to grapple with the impossible choices Black people must make. Mane, even knowing that Pee is making a decision that will cost him his life, tells the listener that if they did it over again, he still wouldn't stop him. Even if Pee didn't make that move that day, he would have to another day. For Pee, it was either make money extralegally or go without food and housing. Mane takes us to the moment of death not to sensationalize violence but to show how it was inevitable. This is less about Pee than about the nature of the South. About how when there are no opportunity structures, Black boys must either die still or walk themselves to their graves. Other Black boys don't stop them because they feel that there is no safe alternative.

This is pain music in the carceral South. Guns and drugs are part of the structural template of the music genre just as guns and drugs are part of the organization of a region that will not tell the truth about its history. These songs tell a narrative about the emotional experiences of Black life in the 252. It is the poetic styling of the sound that produces the vibe, that directs how we feel. When we catch the vibe, our insides tell us what the song is doing. While pain is central to the sound, it is used to create moments and feelings not reducible to it. Out of Black pain come alternative modes of knowing and feeling. This creates the possibility for the South to be more than where it is currently at.

CHAPTER 3

Hanging out the Window with My Ratchet-Ass Friends

Style has a profound meaning to Black Americans. If we can't drive, we will invent walks and the world will envy the dexterity of our feet. If we can't have ham, we will boil chitterlings; if we are given rotten peaches, we will make cobblers; if given scraps, we will make quilts; take away our drums, and we will clap our hands. We prove the human spirit will prevail. We will take what we have to make what we need.
—NIKKI GIOVANNI

When I was a child, my mother planted a garden in the housing projects in the town Amp was murdered in. He wouldn't have remembered this garden. It wasn't memorable. Housing projects in major cities like Chicago and New York have high-rise buildings that pack people beside and on top of each other.[1] In the rural South there is more available land, so the projects aren't single buildings but rather a string of apartments that are connected, forming a cul-de-sac. The buildings in the Weldon projects all look the same. Colorless brick apartments with small cinderblock-colored porches. Each unit is distinguishable only by the patchiness in the grass leading up to it. The design of something tells you how to feel about it. Its purpose in how a thing is built. The Weldon projects felt lifeless. They had only one exit, perimeter patrols, video surveillance, security forces, and police raids. They shared this in common with projects in major cities.

When everything about the landscape was lifeless, my mother created life in the soil little Black children ran barefoot on in the summer, while someone's mother sprayed everyone with a water hose. She planted a garden. There is something to that. Saidya Hartman challenges how we understand the small act of planting a garden in the housing projects when she suggests, "Beauty is not a luxury, rather it is a way of creating possibility in the space of enclosure, a radical act of subsistence, an embrace of our terribleness, a transfiguration of the given."[2] She saw more in the landscape than what it was designed for. In this way beauty isn't what is seen. Most of the flowers that were planted didn't grow or died shortly after. What was beautiful was my mother's attentiveness to the value and glamour in a space assumed to be abject. She allowed tenderness to creep into the soil that others would just step on or look away from. Beauty was the way she pushed back against the violence of it all.

After being notified that she was eligible for public housing assistance, my mother spent three years on the Section 8 waiting list before she was selected to receive housing assistance benefits. What these benefits meant was that my mom, my siblings, and I could go to our house. We didn't have to stay in the projects or in a relative's space. "House" is a seductive term. It evokes the idea of home and belonging, while it dances around terms such as "accessible" and "fundamental." Home is the ways we love on each other in the place that is ours. That place is our house. For some, house is a stand-alone residence that they own. Our Section 8 house was a three-bedroom, two-story apartment that we rented with the financial help of the government. It was brick with a green door, and about twenty other people in my neighborhood had the same looking house as me. Only on the outside, though. When my mom packed all our things and said, "Let's go to our house," she meant it was ours to create, not to own.

We always entered our house from the back door. The front door faced all the apartments in the complex, and the back door gave a sense of privacy. Entering this way brought you in through the kitchen, with the stairs immediately to your left. The bedrooms upstairs were small, which was fine, because it feels good when something that is yours hugs you tight. Those rooms felt like ours until those moments when they didn't. Those moments were random weekdays when my mom would wake us up an hour before our normally scheduled time.

"Make that bed and clean this room before you go to school," she would say.

She would shake my bunkbed to wake my brother and me simultaneously. These mornings my mom felt tense. My room hugged too tightly on these days because I could never seem to fit all my things in it as neatly as my mama wanted. Being twelve years old, I knew that waking up early meant that the housing authorities were coming. I heard my mama yell, "I got my inspection today, and you ain't going to have these folks thinking my house nasty," enough times to know that it mattered to my mama what those state agents thought of her and our house. I didn't know why, though.

I wondered. How could someone my mama didn't like or even know make our house feel like a Section 8 apartment? In the projects my mama had worked hard at using beauty as a barricade between our inner selves and the ugliest that is done to poor Black people. Here the beauty my mama made was still for our protection but not for our consumption. My mother needed to show the housing authority people that she could make beauty in her home, or at least keep it clean, because they had the power to steal our house if she was seen as an unfit mother. My mother created a home that was bound together by cozy rooms and a kitchen that was a room for living. Routinely we had this shattered by the government's surveillance.

This is the experience of many Black women in the 252. This is a carceral experience. Cops, prisons, and other direct contacts with the criminal justice system are the 'heavy hand' of the carceral system. They are the overt ways the South uses surveillance, policing, and control to manage those who are assumed to be negligent and unruly. While contending with these overt systems of power, Black women are also most likely to face the soft hand of the carceral state. Social services and child welfare systems constitute the soft hand of the carceral system in that they use surveillance, policing, and containment, just like the heavy hand, to oversee the people who encounter the system. Dorothy Roberts makes these connections when she shows that when the face of welfare became that of poor Black mothers who society believed had nothing important to impart to their children, the system began to aggressively police Black women, so they would not pass on defiant behaviors to their children.[3] They shattered family bonds, in ways like incarceration. They made houses feel like Section 8 apartments.

My mother and other Black women in the 252 use beauty to push back against the carceral nature of the South. There is style in the way they live. This form of style often challenges ideas of respectability that are centered on motherhood. It challenges ideas that suggest good mothers get their children out of bad neighborhoods or that a good mother wouldn't free her hips and twerk when a song came on that made her feel beautiful. Their beauty and style are more about what Bettina Love calls a "Black ratchet imagination" that centers the emotional and creative flexibility needed to survive state violence in ways that keep one's soul partially intact.[4] They live with the complexities and nuances of working-class Black life. On one hand Black women's creative performances are policed, and on the other it is through attempts at styling value into their lives that they have survived. Beauty is a method. It is the ways Black women style their surroundings that has brought life to them. They have engaged in pain music in a similar fashion. Black women in the 252 have styled pain music with a Black-women-centered epistemology that allows the music to escape the violence of the carceral state through the ways it renegotiates and reimagines mainstream understandings of unruliness and disruptiveness. They style lyrics about guns and drugs with a feminist politic of surviving the day-to-day. Having experienced both the heavy and soft hands of the carceral state, Black women's pain is centered on the multiple ways the South polices and contains. Their music similarly traps the listener within the heaviness of it all.

DOUBLE TIME: LIFE AS SONGLIKE

"In the 252 women rap like men," Lisa says into the phone as I hear her moving around hurriedly. She was getting ready for work when I called early morning to chat about upcoming events and ended up asking her about the type of music women had been putting out in the area recently. Lisa's family moved South to the 252 from New York when she was eleven. Now she works on air at one of the most popular radio stations in the area code.

Trying to keep the conversation at the pace of her moving, she continues and says, "There isn't anything wrong with rapping like men, we all the same. Women be spitting hard, and I like hard rap. They be rapping about drugs and guns, but sometimes women may do a more girly rap."

Lisa alludes to the fact that themes around violence and drugs are popularly viewed as masculine, but she is also destabilizing this by suggesting that there is no inherent difference between men and women. Lisa's understanding is like Donna Troka's contention that the guns we hear cocked in hip-hop songs are often in the hands of women.[5] We have assumed it is a man because when we drew the South, we outlined women as needing protection but never conceived of them providing it.

It was within Lisa's haste of making time for me while also having an exhausting schedule that I felt why trap music was central to Black women in the 252. They live the sound. The rhythmic structure of trap music is double-time. To feel this, count out loud and snap your fingers on each number when you say *one, two, three, four, one, two, three, four.* That's the pace of urgency. Normal time would feel like *one, and, two, and, three, and four.* The ands give you moments of rest that southern Black women are denied.

This is the pulse of a song. Trap sound is complex like the contemporary experiences of southern Black women. They both hold a lot, and surface level readings can't understand the intricacies. While the pulse of trap music is faster than hip-hop was historically, the tempo is slower. The sound accommodates a lot but doesn't feel rushed or compromised in quality. Trap instrumentals are a hybrid of hip-hop and R&B rhythmic elements. Therefore, depending on where you listen and what parts of the song you focus on, it can sound fast, slow, or both simultaneously. This resembles the complexity of the lives of Black women who navigate the South.

Consequently, women can rap hard and soft. Can rap like women but sound like men. Trap is the sound of the experience of making a home in a region that was fertilized by the sweat of your grannies and uncles. Trap is the experience of women and queer people making breathable spaces within a genre that has suffocated its own potential by appropriating the master's tools. All of this is complex. Just as we can hear a trap song as slow or fast, we can also hear the genre as sexist or feminist, depending on where we listen to. At that chicken wing spot in Greenville, Nicole articulated how Black women within the genre lived in double-time or had to put in double the work to carve out a space for themselves.

"There aren't a lot of us women artists," Nicole says. "There really aren't any Black women producers, engineers, or studio owners, and the men always seem to want something from us women to work with us."

The bar in society for men to be viewed as decent is so low that they can quote a few feminist scholars and create a conceptual distance between themselves and the power of patriarchy. Maybe performing this type of feminist politic would have steered the conversation in a way that made it easier for Nicole and me to point out the gendered violence in the 252. But in the moment, I felt I had more in common with the men Nicole was critiquing than I wanted to admit. The men in the 252 were attempting to control the music production, and I was a cis man writing about this gendered web. I was proof of her testimony. I control the narrative.

"What's that like, having to work with men throughout the process of producing your music?" I ask.

Nicole's body opens to face me, and her voice opens just as wide as she goes in detail and says:

A lot of guys don't like when you talk positive about women, and I don't understand that. Why wouldn't you want us to talk positive about ourselves or uplift each other? Because y'all help each other all the time [said in a manner so I would know that I was included] or put out a positive message for males. But when it comes to a woman, y'all think that's crazy or too different. And ask us, "Why would you do that? No one's going to listen to that." I remember one guy told me, "Guys aren't going to listen to that or take that serious because you are talking too positive about women." And I'm like "What?" You would think they would like that women are helping each other, uplifting each other. Even though the song had a positive message too, it was a catchy song.

Nicole describes the ways the hip-hop scene in the 252 can often operate as a "network of misogyny," where the entire structured experience of music making, from the engineers to the male artists, is organized around misogynist behavior.[6] Songs are collective constructions of a locality's art world, and Black women in the 252 have to navigate a system that often does not see Black-women-specific freedom making claims as a legitimate social good.

Remember. In the 252 sound is centered on pain. Black women, who face the heavy and soft hands of the carceral system, are silenced within a space where hurt, anger, and experiences of violence are crucial creative devices. Having their pain and anger silenced by the state and in Black-centered spaces, Black women have used their rage as what Brittney Cooper calls "orchestrated fury."[7] They have learned to take their pain and move through it to build homes, movements, and gestures at new worlds. But just because a skill is useful doesn't mean we should have had to develop it.

My mother's garden was a form of orchestrated fury. She was mad as hell at the unresponsive offices that did not tend to the upkeep of the neighborhood. She was mad as hell at her full-time job at a linen-cleaning factory that did not pay enough to make other housing options possible. So, she did something. Lisa's preference for hard rap that centers on guns is a form of orchestrated fury. There are no systems of accountability built into the South to protect Black women from sexual assault, domestic violence, state violence, and a range of other dangers. I learned this from Imani Perry.[8] From my mother and Mikki Kendall, I understood that Black women are often the only people with an investment in the safety of Black women.[9] Indeed, it makes sense why women like Lisa can emotionally connect with sounds that are anchored in the idea that one's own body is worthy of protecting at any cost. Their daily survival is an embodiment of this type of politic.

Working through and living within double-time provides Black women with new modes of feeling the South. While Aisha S. Durham worked with Black women from the hip-hop generation in the place she calls home, she described her position as the researcher/ed.[10] This is double-time. To be able to recall, remember, and represent a space that is intimate to her in a way that doesn't erase the insides of Black women, she needed a framework to accommodate the complex positionality of Black women. Double-time isn't about doing and being multiple things at once. Rather, it pushes back against the controlling images and stereotypes that flatten Black women's humanity to justify various forms of violence. These narratives suggest that Black women can't shake ass and be a good mother. They can't rap about carrying guns and have access to femininity. Double time reconciles these incompatibilities and suggests that these contradictory ways of being aren't contradictory. If we can admit that Black women can be more than flat archetypes, then we must question how we have justified systems of violence toward them.

Brit, a 252 local, wore the complexity of this experience on her body. I pick her up from her job at the county department of social services, where she helps residents get access to government assistance. She wanted to show me a hole-in-the-wall diner. Since the diner didn't have a website that I could get the address from, and she knew how to get there only through muscle memory, we decided to ride together. She steps in on the passenger side of my car left foot first, and I notice her cardigan that covers both of her shoulders. Today she looks like someone who works at the social services office. We walk into the small restaurant that has around eight small tables that can accommodate two or three people each. I follow her as she stands in what looks like a catering line. On the other side of the line are two short, older Black women who have mastered using the word "baby" to welcome and calm people of all ages. They are scooping food from silver catering pans that looks as if it was prepared by the women serving. That food that is made with granny's love. But also with the pain in her back and fingers from working all her life. The food that has no recipe, you just keep seasoning it until it feels like it is enough. It was one of those places.

"Glad to be out the office," she says as we walk our plates piled with chicken and white rice and gravy to our table.

"Rough day?" I ask.

"Folks just don't know how to do stuff, so my job is harder than it has to be," she says. I shake my head, indicating I know the feeling, while I taste the sweet tea in my Styrofoam cup.

Brit is twenty-six years old and moved back to the 252 after college to be close to family. She imagined that working at the department of social services would be a way to give back to her community with her degree. Her frustration today, while we eat food that is so good that it should always be eaten in good company, is the same frustration she feels every other day. Her clients, mainly Black women, don't often know the protocol or paperwork for the services they are seeking. This creates moments where angered Black women seeking support for their families must collide with just-as-frustrated Black women who are on the front lines in social services departments, who are also struggling to take care of their families.

"It be confusing, all the hoops you have to jump through just for clients to get a little help," she says. "I work there so I understood what I had to do to get my assistance." Brit's experience is one of double-time or the complex sets of positions Black women embody that produce multiple ways of hearing and knowing space. She both works at and receives benefits from the department of social services. A government resource that is popularly understood as supporting working-class families reproduces a Black underclass by not paying its employees enough for them to live independent of the services they provide to others. Brit is a provider and receiver of government assistance. She works for a system that does harm and is also harmed by it.

The spectacle of carcerality is often the white male cop killing the unarmed Black person. The violence of it is evident. The long wait times, unclear procedures, and intrusive practices of social service and welfare systems are everyday forms of violence. The violence that isn't evident may be more likely to kill us. The violence of social service and welfare systems is an extension of police violence, and the face of these systems in rural Black towns is not white men. It is often Black women who answer the phones, handle the cases, and wo(man) the front desks in these departments. Forced with few economic opportunities, Brit shows the inescapability of structural violence in the South.

The normative organization of the system does harm. Brit says, "I have to cut corners just so some people don't starve. I feel what they be going through." I didn't ask what she meant by cutting corners, because I did not want her to feel she needed to compromise her clients or herself. Honestly, I didn't have to. I knew it was those moments that she pushed back against the rules that harm Black women like her. Under her brown cardigan were tattoos that showed her commitments. She greeted me with her social services voice, but after a few minutes of conversation she curved her vowels in a tone no different than my mother. It was the way that she bent the rigid regulations of her job that changed the texture of experience for the Black women she serviced. It is within this process of cutting, bending, and remixing that Black woman make breathable moments within the carceral

South. They change the vibe of spaces. Black women in the 252 have created beauty in painful moments. They bent and styled pain music and painful experiences to produce a sound and vibe that centers rural Black women's subjectivity. To understand the music, we first had to talk through the way Black women's lives are musiclike.

BEATING DOWN YO BLOCK

To hear the 252, I often had to leave the 252. Larger venues in major cities were assumed to offer a form of glamour that was not accessible in small rural towns. Venues in the 252 were small and brought out sounds and faces that were familiar. Artists would share music that held the darkest parts of their softest selves, that was recorded in even darker rooms that were referred to as local studios. In these dark rooms, weed smoke and dreams always filled the air. Both made these small studios feel more snug than tight. Given these venues were filled with community members, the events often felt like a wake. It was people you were close to and familiar with listening to narrations of death, pain, and hope. Performing at events in Raleigh and Charlotte provided the opportunity to see if these experiences were fashioned in ways that they could enter the ears and pores of those outside of home and make them feel something.

One Saturday a venue in Raleigh is holding an event showcasing the top artists in eastern North Carolina. The only woman on the event flyer is Ivy. Ivy was born and raised in the 252. She wears color on her body and lips. As a twenty-six-year-old that looks no older than twenty-two, her choice in blazers and jewelry gives her a mature vibe that her youthful face hadn't yet captured. I drive a little under an hour and a half on Highway 95 and Highway 40 to get to Raleigh from Halifax County. I go solo, hoping the awkwardness of standing alone will push me to engage with new faces.

I walk into a slightly lit bar with the stage immediately to my left. Folks are standing with drinks in hands and eyes pointed to the stage, waiting for the first artist to go on. Ten minutes in the venue, and I see Ivy near the bar in the back. I feel like this isn't the right time, but I walk to her and greet her.

"I'm looking forward to your performance," I say. Sounds just as corny on paper as it did in person.

She gives me an abrupt but polite "thank you," letting me know she wanted that to be the extent of the conversation. Her response was in part due to her needing to prepare for her set and because of Nicole's earlier assertion that men always want something from women artists. Not to push too hard, I give her a fifteen-second summary of my project to explain my presence. She smiles while saying, "Oh, I thought you were . . . I understand." We exchange contact info before she heads toward the DJ booth.

Ivy's hesitancy toward me was more than a mere single instance of not wanting to be bothered but speaks to a larger process in which Black women artists must strategically navigate the music economy. Black women's emotions, and thus their ability to produce pain music, are overshadowed by patriarchy's reach into the rural South. The endurance Black women have developed to survive the South doesn't seem like endurance, just survival. We miss the creative and radical modes of being that make living possible for Black feminine-identifying people. Ivy and others are accustomed to men approaching them under the guise of music to gain sexual and emotional companionship. When artists like Ivy develop a sizeable reputation, men want to be connected to their music-making process. In both situations Black women's value lies within how much it meets the needs of men. Her hesitancy toward me was grounded in not wanting her subjectivity to be consumed by my immediate needs, academic or otherwise.

I feel nervous. Because Ivy was right in her hesitancy. I'm not sure if I can hold up the weight of the story. Maybe all stories benefit the writer in ways they can't who is being written about. I'm not sure if there is any string of words a Black cis man could weave together to allow a reader to feel the experience of being with your people, working in a tradition that supposedly carves out spaces of refuge for your community, and doing the thing that makes living worth living, and in that space you still feel that to be heard you must lose all the pieces of your voice that serve you selfishly. This is what underpinned Ivy's hesitancy.

There is something honest about how Ivy and others were responding to this. In 2018 the "scammer" took center stage in southern Black women's hip-hop. City Girls and Megan Thee Stallion had women and men alike across the world rapping lyrics that used the imagery of women scamming men for material gain without any regard to men's feelings. For Diana Khong, Black women use the aesthetics of the scammer as a restorative figure, because the objectification of men works as a counterpoint to the dominant gender and capitalist structure.[11] If the rules of the world are always to the emotional and material benefit of men, then for Black women, the scammer is an attempt to gain material autonomy while holding on to the softest parts of themselves.

A year before the scammer took center stage internationally, Ivy released a song called M.O.N. (Money Over Niggas) as a women's independence single. The narrative song asks women to value their own self-sustaining over men's egos. Pushing back against the notion that Black women must invest in Black

men's potential and stick with them through material and emotional hard-
ships at the expense of their own personal well-being, Ivy raps, "Tell him he
second while money is first / Then walk away with his ego in your purse."[12]
Ivy is working in the scamming aesthetic with other Black women in the
South to suggest that scamming does not only take back economic resources
but undercuts the systems that preserve the emotional power of men. Some
say women are more emotional than men. Really, men's emotions organize
systems. This renders them invisible. When women walk off with men's egos
in their purses, they are weakening a system that demands men live for their
own emotional gratitude and asking them to *feel* in community with others.
It is asking men to feel differently.

Two lines into Ivy's performance, and the predominately male audience
does a collective "ayyyeee," as communal hand signals are thrown in the air
and heads start bobbing. Her flow is different from most in the 252. Most
artists here have a melodic rap style, but her first two lines touched my skin
the same as when I heard Biggie's "Juicy" for the first time—you could feel
the weight of the hood being soothed by the beauty of Black people. Her
flow didn't sound like the 252, but it felt like it. What I mean is that her flow
was crisper and more precise than most 252 artists. She punched at the end
of lines, while 252 artists sang the end of theirs. But her flow couldn't mask
that she curled her syllables the way the 252 does when we need to get our
point across. The way she said "granny" sounded like both a person and
space of refuge. There was something familiar in her performance that the
crowd could feel.

I wanted to understand how Ivy could make me feel at home with a sound
from up North. Weeks later we were able to have a brief chat. When I brought
up her rap delivery, she responded, "My style as an artist is raw. My flow is
more like the New York spitters." In this way Ivy distances herself from the
more harmonic southern style.[13] In an interview on her YouTube channel
advertising the Spoken Gunz Female Cypher, Ivy cites Fabolous and Biggie as
two of her biggest influencers in developing her passion for hip-hop culture
and her flow.[14] A lot of women artists, like Ivy, use a continuous free-flowing
delivery style, as this rhythm structures the vibe of the song around notions
of seriousness and toughness.

"Ladies actually have to rap," she tells me.

Ivy is in double-time. Since women are often overlooked, she developed
an intricate and distinctive rhyming technique while also performing local
sensibilities. She had to make contradictions not contradictions. She was
able to make a sound not associated with this region feel like it was. Men in
the 252 lean on autotune to produce a melodic flow that stresses pain, but

Black women have worked to master different flows to stake claim in what is popularly assumed to be a male-centered space. They have expanded ways to feel home.

Flow is honest. There are no set, rigid boundaries that separate men and women's flows. Flow doesn't conform to gendered binaries. In thinking about the way rappers' flows push the boundaries of how we understand personal subjectivity, Elaine Richardson asks, "How do rappers display, on the one hand, an orientation to their situated, public role as performing products, and, on the other, that their performance is connected to discourses of authenticity and resistance?"[15] A flow is good when it can make contradictions not contradictions. It must perform both a social position and individuality. It must connect you to a community and distinguish you from it. It must be familiar and fresh. In this way when I say "Black women's flow in the 252," I am not naming a similar sound but rather a collective of stylistic choices that hit the eardrum in ways that expand and complicate our understanding of Black women's experiences in the region. Their sound isn't static but always in motion. It's those sounds that allow us to say with a level of honesty that we hear and feel the region from Black women's social experience.

Ivy's flow broke away from the melodic southern flow used by many artists in the region. This did not tear her away from being able to produce sounds that felt sincerely 252. Women like Redd carved their flow out within the melodic rap delivery space. While Ivy and Redd approach their flow differently, their music dances and flirts with each other in ways that make it meaningful to think about them under the umbrella of a Black woman's 252 style. You can do the same choreography to different songs. Similarly, Ivy and Redd both offer us different sonic experiences, but the vibe of their music moves our insides in similar ways.

Redd is a twenty-five-year-old queer woman who was born and raised in the 252. She has light brown skin and dreads that fall to the center of her T-shirt. I was able to catch Redd in Roanoke Rapids at an outdoor concert showcasing local artists. Artists rented out a community center that is typically used for parties and wedding receptions, and used the outside space to hold the event. I arrived early. I couldn't stay long, so I got there a few minutes before the event began. The artists organizing the event were still setting up, so I knew I probably wouldn't see any performances. It was as if everyone knew the time on the flyer was the time that set-up would begin and not the time that the show would start, because only one other person not organizing the event was there. I forgot that Black folks communicate that way sometimes.

To make the outside space not feel as big and awkward, I walk up to Redd to chat while she is chilling to the side. We have some familiarity from Facebook. We are not familiar enough that my conversation would be expected, but close enough to where it didn't feel completely out of the blue.

"How you feeling?" I ask, making room for Redd to address her performance, the heat, or anything on her mind that could be squeezed into small talk.

"I'm doing good, can't complain," she responds. Often most people respond to "How you feeling?" with "Good," because it is not customary to open a conversation with a barrage of complaints. Even though people say they are good, it is within the cadence of how "good" is spoken that their honest feelings are. Redd seemed to be well and excited about the show. After light conversation I ask about how it feels to be the only woman in the show.

"Rap is the same as anything else," she says. "It's just like playing basketball, I guess. It is looked at as a predominately male thing, so as a woman you have to be on your A1 at all times. Bring your best game because people constantly looking at you and judging you because you are a woman."

Suggesting that the exclusion and denial Black women face in rap is "like everything else" is Redd's way of calling out the everydayness of violence toward Black women. Treva B. Lindsey calls this "unlivable living."[16] This is the way multiple systems of disadvantage compound to produce spaces that harm the life chances of Black women. Even in intercollegiate basketball, we judge women's performances based on how much they overlap with men's play style.[17] There are no readily available frameworks to hold Black women and make sense of where they are in this world. Rap, just like everything else, is structured to disadvantage Black women, and Black women have often responded by doing what Gwendolyn Pough calls "bringing wreck."[18] This sounds fitting when it is everything that needs to be torn down. For Pough, bringing wreck is when Black women are talking back or turning up.[19] It is how their words bend airwaves in ways that add oxygen into suffocating spaces. Assumptions about Black women's criminality would have us believe that bringing wreck is always loud and violent. Although it often is and should be, bringing wreck in the 252 can also be creative and imaginative processes for Black women.

Redd brings wreck in the 252 by using the flow of the region but doing it in ways men can't. She points to this when she says, "I had to create my own wave inside the sound. I got that trap soul flow." Most artists in the region work from a melodic rap delivery, and Redd has called hers trap soul. For Redd, she wrecks the structure of the 252 musical scene by sitting within the sound of the region and carving and slicing a space within it that can hold the softest parts of herself. Voices can never be lost, only silenced. As a queer Black woman from the South, she has always had something to say. The task was to make legible who she was within a tradition that, as Mark Anthony Neal says, "marked gay *somebodies* as cultural strangers."[20] She is beating down the block. "Beating down the block" can mean a variety of things at a variety of different moments. Here, I am using it to point to moments of staking physical and sonic ownership of space. Redd's sound stayed home. She took the sounds that filled the streets of the place she calls home and rescripted them to render queer 252 identity legible. By mastering what was denied to her, she wrecked the dominant scripts of who trap is supposed to be in service of. In different ways both Ivy and Redd had to beat down the block to push back against the gendered narratives of what and where the trap sound is. This is where Black women's sound is located. Within the stylistic choices Black women make to create themselves as both woman and 252. When it is everything that is violent, the normality of society must be beaten, rescripted, and restructured. What better place to start than your own block?

WE HOPPIN' OUT AT RED LIGHTS, TWERKIN' ON THEM HEADLIGHTS

I heard Black femme-presenting people talk about unequal systems. Their stories made happiness feel like a break from pain. Pain was always there. They talked about desires of survival. But I rarely heard the word "feminist." There was always a feminist politic at play. This allowed mothers to make it from Tuesday to payday with only fifteen dollars. Women pushed back against their children being suspended from school for being children. This is feminist. These may have required less-than-legal ways of making money, and raising your voice at school officials, but all of it is underpinned by a feminist politic of surviving the structural violence of the day-to-day. When the term "feminist" was invoked in conversations, most were not opposed to the term, but rather it seemed that no one had a stake in the rhetorical possibilities of the term. Identifying or not identifying with it. Salvaging or dismissing the term. None of these choices would solve the structural conditions of everyday life.

The ambivalence toward feminism as a concept was less about the politic of it—they lived feminist as praxis—but a pushback against the respectability of mainstream conceptions and misrepresentations of what a liberating feminist politic demanded. White liberal feminism that centered on women freeing themselves from the family structure, moving into the workforce, and using policing to fix transgressions against women, didn't fit within the day-to-day needs of the women in the 252. These responses rely on the assumption that society sees Black women as women. That they have selves that can be defended. To be seen as worthy always fall back on being some form of respectable. Mikki Kendall says that respectability "requires erasing your memory of how it felt to be hungry, cold, scared, and so on until all that is left is a placid surface to mask the raging maelstrom underneath."[21] Respectability is the lie we tell rural poor Black woman, that if they can endure suffering gracefully, something or someone will see them as worth saving.

Ivy is one of the leading voices on women's liberation in the 252. Rather than pace back and forth within the cage of respectability, she offers a feminist politic in double-time. Her song is both slow and fast. Violent and loving. Destructive and resilient. It just depends on where we listen. Take this excerpt from her song "Roll in Peace":

> I just want to roll in peace, but bitches be thinking I'm weak,
> 'Cuz I stay cooking in every kitchen I walk in, but I'm never in beef.[22]

Ivy is working through the trap genre specifically alluding to drug dealing. She engages in this scheme in a gendered manner. "Roll in peace" alludes to a double entendre from rapper Kodak Black suggesting she can't chill in her city because everyone knows her, and alludes to not being able to comfortably roll a blunt because of police activity. "But bitches be thinking I'm weak," refers to men and women assuming she is soft and nonconfrontational, likely due to her feminine-presenting image. The following line, "'Cuz I stay cooking in every kitchen I walk in," is a gendered double entendre that is a play on the idea that a woman's place is the kitchen, but she is simultaneously referencing cooking crack. She is bridging gendered expectations with the expectations of the trap. She finishes by stating "but I'm never in beef," which for her is a gendered double entendre letting us know that she is in the kitchen, but she isn't handling food and that her status is too important to be in continuous competition with someone else.

Ivy is destabilizing the masculine undertones of trap by styling the content with gendered aesthetics. She is pushing back against a system where gender tells us more about what we can't do than can. Gender is less about providing us roles than about foreclosing them. To put it plainly, Ivy is saying that she wants to chill and smoke to deal with the heaviness of it all. Not because she wants to be like men, but because she just wants to be. This is feminist. Feminist critique doesn't have to be scholarly. It can be hood. When it is hood, it unlocks a range of queer possibilities that scholarly and other positively perceived texts cannot. Racquel Gates suggests that "negative texts open up possibilities for nonnormative feelings, experiences, and allegiances that are not possible in the image-policed spaces of positive texts."[23] Texts that push back against respectability and acceptable ways of being offer modes of feminist feeling and possibility that are not available through normative frameworks. Trap music is perceived by the dominant culture as negative, specifically because of its emphasis on drugs and violence. Rather than argue that drug and gun lore is positive, Ivy and others demonstrate that there can be productive feminist value in negative texts. The gendered double entendre makes it possible to be both woman and hood. To feel that you can both physically defend yourself and are worthy of being defended by others. Respectability benefits only the systems that cause the pain.

When systems control the ways in which you respond to them, it no longer matters how you feel and live within them. Only the narrowest form of critique will be possible. Within the logics of respectability, Black women don't even have to win to be punished, but as Kiese Laymon says, "all they have to do is not lose the way white people want them to."[24] Structurally, Black women are at constant threat of carceral and interpersonal violence, and this is maintained by forcing Black women to rely on the language and logics of these systems as their only form of redress. Trap music, pain music specifically, provides a mode of feeling beyond these logics. It embraces rage, anger, fury, and pain. These nonnormative feelings provide the opportunity to feel the queerness of it all.[25] Black women's feelings are positioned as out of place if they don't serve the prevailing social order. Hood, ratchet, and trap sensibilities are analytical sites to help make sense of the way patriarchy and racism always dance with each other.

If we look at Redd's song "Cutter," we can see the way queer Black women bend and style trap music to expand our understanding of feminist possibility. The song can make us feel otherwise and differently. "Mama will tell you I ain't ever been nice, never been the type to play with these niggas / Bruh just bought him a brand new cutter, ready to chop shit down ain't playing with these niggas / That cutter go chop chop / I been on the opp block / My shit like hotspot. Turn a tee into a crop top."[26] This song narrates owning a weapon and naming it a cutter because of the way it cuts through skin. In this verse Redd starts by pushing back against the "nice little girl" trope, the notion that girls' value lies in their ability to be compassionate toward others. In narrating being willing to use violence against those who aim to do violence to her, she gives the image that this violence is directed toward men in that she will turn a normal-sized male shirt into a crop top, which is typically worn by women.

To put this in context, first we must acknowledge that Black women are more likely to be victims of gun violence than all other women. In a society where elementary-school shootings have not moved the country to feel differently about gun laws, the right to a weapon is a core piece of how the US imagines itself. The US values the idea of using a weapon to protect oneself. But when it is Black, queer, woman, and other socially nonnormative bodies being protected, guns are understood as violent, not liberatory. By this I mean that when violence is in service of the social order, we don't call it violence but call it supporting the troops or Veterans Day. When violence is in service of queer bodies, violence is central to how we make sense of the moment. It is not that Redd is wholesale advocating for violence. Rather, she is working within and against dominant sexual and racial ideologies. If the US rhetorical use of violence is aimed at imperial freedom, and Black men's use of violence is aimed at racial justice, then when the voice of violence is queered, it is an indictment of all the various systems that converge to do harm to all othered bodies. Hearing Redd's voice carve out a cadence that is neither feminine nor masculine and push back against the notion that women must be idle receivers of abuse produces the possibility to feel alternative modes of survival. Nonnormative bodies can be seen as *somebody*.

Carceral logics police not only the physical and material reality of Black women's lives but also the types of responses that can be made in response to these structures.[27] Black women in the 252 push back against the carceral nature of respectability through styling trap songs in ways that capture the complexity of life in the South. The stylistic choices they make reflect their gendered emotional histories. It reflects a desire to be hood, ratchet, street and not have that foreclose their ability to live nuanced gendered lives. The goal is not only to survive, but to do it with style. With a style that encompasses the range of possibilities that live within the body that the style is draped on.

QUEERING THE GUN

My head hurts. In this chapter about gender performance in the 252, I have not spoken about masculinity. To do so honestly, I will inevitably have to say something about myself. While the lives of Black men who were kind enough to open their inner worlds to me will guide the conversation, I don't want their stories to mask my own bullshit. What I mean by is this that I don't want to offer critique of them without showing how I am also implicated within unhealthy performances. Scholarship should never cover the ways we struggle to be honest about our desires and performances. None of the men I work with openly identified as queer, nor do I. But I do want to tell a brief story about Black masculinity in the 252 from a Black queer and feminist lens. Specifically, thinking with Jeffrey Q. McCune Jr.'s contention that "the frequency of black death is itself queer."[28] In the South, Black people and their bodies are always out of place. Never fully home. Constantly made a spectacle. For Black men in the 252, death feels like it sits in the room with us, or at least it's around the corner. Within this context Black men in the South have strived for beauty, intimacy, and the erotic, even when they have not had a language to name it as such. Black men have queered the sound of US life, or as Durell M. Callier suggests, they live in C minor.[29] The minor chords are the black keys on the piano, which bring in darker, smoother, soulful sounds that push back against the normality of the major chords.[30] There is a queerness to cis Black men's search for softness. We can better understand this search in conversation with differently positioned bodies to see how much and how little bodies can tell us.

A few weeks into my senior year of high school, my close friend Zay purchased a Toyota Camry for around $1,000. I was partly envious of his newfound freedom, but mostly excited that I would get to experience this freedom with him. This freedom wasn't solely about movement— we could get a parent to drop us off anywhere—but about who we got to be when we got places. We no longer had to stand outside the movie theater and wave at girls who passed, hoping one would take the motion of my hand going side-to-side as an invitation to go in and watch a movie together. We could sit in the car in the movie theater parking lot with the windows down and cut on the newest T.I. album and invite folks over to vibe with us. Car culture provides a ritualized entry into adulthood where Black boys make sense of beauty, prestige, and style. When talking about his car, Zay found a piece of his voice that was lodged deep down behind his left rib cage where words like "gorgeous" and "delicate" are stored. Owning a car wasn't just about getting places, but it was one of the first times Zay could make something sound and look beautiful and still have access to the idea of manhood that is packaged and sold to young Black boys in the hood. I never heard Zay call himself beautiful. I did hear him say that about his car. I know that he had a desire to make *something* sound and look like love was put in it. Even when he was unsure if his body deserved this type of care.

Through his fast-food job, Zay was able to save up enough money to buy some rims for his $1,000 Camry. I'm not sure how much the rims cost, but I would assume at minimum they were half of what he paid for the vehicle. At the time, Zay was a hip-hop artist and wanted a sound system that could do justice to the sounds he recorded in his bedroom. I think he wanted everyone to hear him just as much as he wanted the car. Zay was able to buy a stereo and sound system for a few hundred dollars and installed it himself. When dominant narratives about being a man led us to believe that masculinity was about how easily we could break something and how much we could bend without breaking, Zay was gentle with his car. He loved his car and shared what he loved with me. I loved him because of it. This is intimacy. We both had a desire to make things beautiful and to make that space between us and other Black boys into something that felt like love.

When I returned south for fieldwork and saw Hondas with nineteen-inch rims and "lit" painted on the side, I thought about the type of care that went into those choices. Care is attention to detail. During my fieldwork my oldest brother, Wink, purchased a car for $900 and immediately he began looking online for rims.

"I just drive it to work, but when it gets right, I might drive it on the weekend," he says while I watch him scroll his phone looking at used rims.

"What's wrong with it?" I ask.

"It run good. Just doesn't have a radio right now. I need to fix her up," he says.

For my brother, the car he just purchased was currently important only for utility: to get him to work. In the rural South, there is no public transportation, so everyone drives or borrows rides. In driving economies vehicles are important aspects of social engagement.[31] My brother knew this. His car revealed something about him.

A major normative assumption would be that it is more rational to buy a $2,000 car than to spend $900 on a cheap car and $1,000 for it to meet aesthetic standards.[32] But my brother was working in C minor. He was trying to produce a smooth and soulful feeling through the way his body moved across the landscape. In thinking through how hip-hop has allowed the Black community in the 252 to perform gender, I understand the importance of buying the $900 car and putting expensive rims on it the same way that I argue we should read hip-hop performance and lyrical content. Derek Iwamoto contends that mainstream society misunderstood Tupac's importance because they engaged his music and performative behavior as literal representations, which did not allow them to see how Tupac's work was a matter of gendered style rather than simply substance.[33] My brother would rather spend additional money on creating a car that would draw attention because of its aesthetics than spend money on a car with a more reliable engine and transmission because his car allowed him to perform a particular style of masculinity: repositioning the substantive value of what's under the hood. Destabilizing substantive value and privileging aesthetics has a long tradition in Black aesthetics, with William De Vaughn saying, "You may not have a car at all, but you can still stand tall."[34] Thinking at the intersections of Black car and hip-hop culture opens up a space to engage with the types of gendered narratives that can be constructed by centering the style of hip-hop performativity, rather than engaging with the lyrics and behaviors of 252 artists solely as literal representations of who they are or want to be. Instead of engaging merely with what is being said, examining the way in which artists aesthetically and poetically make statements within the trap genre can point us to new understandings of gendered subjectivity.

Zay's and my brother's stories challenge the masculine master narrative around car culture and show that it can be a queer experience. The culture isn't really about the car itself but about the ways these men can touch something and it can become beautiful. The way they can find styles, designs, and sounds that bend and expand the body of the car. The best cars are the most queered ones. Similarly, trap music isn't inherently about the lyrics, but rather the way beauty, pain, and color can be added to them. It's the way lyrics are dressed up that they are made to mean. Style then becomes a way in which meaning becomes structured into a vibe. Style refers not only to a particular way in which something is done but is a key component of what that something is. Cars are some of the only bodies Black men in the South feel they have the freedom to dress and make up. The desire to make a body beautiful is there, even when they feel that it can't be their own. Similarly, it is behind gun lyrics that Black men in the South have felt the most comfortable speaking their pain and desires. The gun is the microphone, and vulnerability is the song.

THEY THINK I'M PUSSY 'CAUSE I SING A LITTLE BIT, BITCH, I'M DANGEROUS

While sitting beside Shell on his living room couch, he says, "Singing doesn't make you soft. It just shows you have more to offer as an artist." His cousin sits on the floor across the room from us with his back on the front door, listening to Shell describe himself. Shell is around 5'5" and his wide-eye glass frames add an eclectic feel to his ripped jeans and Timberland boots. We all sit in Shell's mother's living room talking and taking momentary breaks in the conversation, when Shell's niece shyly pokes her head into the living room for a little attention.

"Do you sing on a lot of your songs?" I ask after one of her visits.

Letting go of his soft tone, his voice gets heavier when he says, "Yes. I add some vocals to most tracks. I can actually sing, though."

Shell doesn't sound defensive but honest. He wants me to know that he values the melodic pieces of his sound. This is not new. Southern rappers have always challenged the singer-rapper binary, and trap rappers have normalized incorporating singing vocals and adlibs over their beats, with Atlanta rapper Future being one of the most notable.[35] Even when rappers can't sing, auto-tune will be used to get the pitch right, because a melodic flow is important to the genre. Shell's assertion "I can actually sing, though" is his attempt to say something about his sound. He is in conversation with the idea that all rappers sing a little on their songs but wants me to know that his singing is crafted with honesty and skill.

My body feels like it has been here before. It sits deep inside Shell's couch as if the couch were already familiar with my curves. Usually when I am unfamiliar with the pictures on the walls of the room, my body sits on the edge of my seat trying not to become too entangled with chairs that don't know how to hold me just yet. It is the way Shell's humble and kind personality made the couch, pictures on the wall, and sound of a small person's feet running feel like I was welcome to experience these pieces of home as a distant relative and not as a new guest.

While feeling the warmth Shell created in the room with his vibe, it was when he discussed singing that I felt like I was getting closer to how he imagined himself. His vowels curled differently. His words were more pointed and direct. While he is discussing how he has merged both his rapping and singing ability he says, "They don't see what we do as art, they hear the robbing and shooting and don't see the craft."

I'm not sure who "they" are in this statement. Maybe "they" are white people. Possibly it is those people who blame crime and violence on hip-hop. Whoever "they" are, Shell believes they hear the lyrics but not the voice. There is something within the cadence, the gasps for air, and strained vocal cords that when combined with robbing and shooting lyrics produces a piece of art that is qualitatively different than the individual parts. This is why Tricia Rose named her book *Black Noise*. "They" don't have a frame to grapple with the polyvocal dimensions of hip-hop and have not been able to hear the love, pain, and range of emotional possibilities that rap creates.[36] "They" hear noise. "They" don't hear or feel the multiple emotional subjectivities Shell is embodying by queering his voice. Singing in and of itself is not queer, but rather Shell's emphasis on sounding otherwise or differently is. He is pushing back against folks refusing to see his voice as a carrier of meaning. In the hood Black men's voices crack and break. They also sing. It is the desire to have all these pieces heard as legitimate that is important for Shell.

Telling me about his singing doesn't feel sincere to Shell. He turns his body so we both are looking in the same direction and puts his cell phone in front of both of us. I'm always uncomfortable listening to a song on the spot. What if I don't like it? What if I do like it but lack the vocabulary to explain why in a way that the artist and I can share a moment together? Shell plays his song "Say Goodbye." The first thing I notice is that the song starts with the drums stripped from the beat, and a soft timbre that has a heartfelt vibe. About twenty-five seconds in, Shell's voice comes on alongside hi-hats and kick drums to use the trap structure to add texture to the song. He rap-sings throughout the verses by holding notes at the end of each bar. At the end of the second verse, Shell pulls out the drums and uses a decrescendo when he raps, "One shot, to the face / He's suffering from gunshots to the face / I'm feeling it and only got one stop to you babe / You all I need in this life / I still got demons to fight." Listening, I'm not sure who is doing the shooting and who is being shot. All that is clear is that some form of violence occurred. There is love too.

Holding the weight of his childhood in his throat, Shell tells me this song is about his best friend who was murdered when they were twelve. I never know how to comfort people in these moments when sympathy feels like pity, empathy feels like appropriation, and sharing your own trauma feels like decentering the other person.

"This is a tough thing to carry around as a child," he says. "But I knew people either wouldn't understand or would overwhelm me by feeling sorry for me, so I never spoke about this until this song."

It seemed as if Shell let me in on a secret. Secrets are not things that people don't know, but rather things that can't be spoken above silence without something or someone breaking.

Shell's response is twofold in that Black boys feel their environment isn't structured to understand their emotional needs, and Black boys often feel they don't deserve to be too emotionally cared for. For Black men in the South, the carceral experience isn't just police sirens and handcuffs but the many ways Black men's emotional capacity is surveilled and imprisoned by dominant conceptions of masculinity. bell hooks says, "Whether in an actual prison or not, practically every Black male in the United States has been forced at some point in his life to hold back the self he wants to express, to repress and contain for fear of being attacked, slaughtered, destroyed."[37] Just as prison cells produce tough-guy personas and violence, the notion of an idealized masculinity serves as a carceral constraint that debilitates Black men's emotional possibilities.

It was only when the hi-hats and 808s masked the silence of the everyday that Shell was comfortable sharing his secret with me. The grittiness and heaviness of the trap bass produced a space to share something intimate where he was confident no one would break. If he did happen to break down, the tempo, instrumentation, and lyrical content of the trap structure could hold him up. Shell falls back on his use of vocals to sing about pain in a song that superficially has heavy violent undertones. It is the heavy bass, gun and drug lore, and darkness of the trap sound that free Shell to queer his voice to work through his gendered-emotional subjectivity. The dark sound and guns are what builds the genre, but rather it is Shell's fluctuation in voice, search for pitch, and vocal pauses that gesture toward something honest about his feelings in the song. All trap songs work within the trap structure; it is how they are styled that produces the vibe of the song.

Redd was on to something when she said basketball is like everything else. In the 1992 film *White Man Can't Jump*, Billy, the white protagonist, critiques his Black teammate Sidney by telling him, "You'd rather look good and lose than look bad and win." What Billy didn't see was that Sidney lived in a neighborhood plagued with violence and always had to portray tough-ness, while codeswitching at his job to not offend his white boss so that he could save up to move his family out of that neighborhood. Living through his style on the court made up some of the few moments we saw Sidney sincerely be himself. Similarly, it is within the aesthetic choices Black men make while producing pain music where we get a glimpse of how Black men in the South are attempting to make sense of their emotional subjectivity in ways not overly determined by the carceral system. Using style to sound and feel beyond rigid dominant conceptions of manhood is an attempt at a more liberating masculinity.

GUNS AIN'T MASCULINE, THE WAY I TALK ABOUT THEM IS

"I would shoot a porno if I could get paid for it," TDot says.

We both explode with laughter. While fighting back the hysterics, I ask him to explain. TDot and I generally hang out in the parking lot of his apart-ment complex. We use his car to hold drinks and our bodies when we need to lean against something to give our legs a break from supporting our full heaviness. As both a hip-hop artist and videographer, TDot has worked with a wide range of artists in the area in multiple capacities.

"I'm just saying a camera can be used multiple ways, and since it's not a lot available around here I have to be creative with my resources."

"I feel you," I say while still laughing about the initial comment.

"Nobody's hiring, but I have to make money," he says. "I got my car so I can be like a taxi. I will pick you up for $10 or I will come help you pick up your groceries. Even clean your crib. I'm able to get there because I drive, you feel me. Being a man is about making it happen."

For TDot being a man is about making things happen by pushing back against the structural conditions you find yourself in and making something else possible.

TDot's understanding of masculinity often falls in line with Mark Anthony Neal's term "Strong Black Man" where Black men, in the face of white supremacy, aim to provide financial support, discipline, and honor to their families, while also publicly being chivalrous to Black women.[38] It is within them that Black liberation is made possible. In a society that deems Black men as criminal and lazy, the strong Black man embodies a spirit of thrift that will uplift the Black community. This static and one-dimensional form of masculinity sometimes negates the bright, eccentric, and visceral masculinities that are lived with and alongside other types of bodies. The strong Black man ideal relies on heteronormative and patriarchal assumptions and forecloses softness, queerness, and a range of other modes of being for Black men. The Black community does not need benevolent strong Black men to lead us, but rather men who will reach down into their inner selves and realize the stuff that makes up the depths of them *feel* just like the insides of other gendered and nongendered bodies.

TDot complicates a binary understanding between being a strong Black man and embodying progressive masculinity. I think I do too.

"Men need more masculinity in their music. And adding how many guns you own isn't making it masculine either," TDot exclaims as he is talking to me about how he understands the relationship between his identity and music. He challenges the popular idea that guns and violence in hip-hop are solely male-centered tropes. A white liberal feminism would reduce gun and drug lyrics in trap music to hypermasculinity. While hypermasculinity may be part of the equation, it leaves us with an unfinished understanding of the emotional and aesthetic nuances made by both women and men who work within this genre. I doubt that TDot was making room to include Black women's role in the genius of the trap genre, but he is pushing back against the idea that weapons make a man a man.

As TDot made this comment critiquing the conflation of guns with masculinity, his most recent single, entitled "Free Smoke," opens with him rapping, "Free smoke, free smoke / Unload, reload / These niggas, they don't know me." In pushing TDot a little, I ask, "Doesn't your music talk about guns?"

"Yeah, but I actually be talking about stuff with it," he responds.

I wanted to make sense of this, because I know TDot's politics, and he would give his camera up for his community. He was kind. He always held himself accountable to the best of his ability. TDot, an avid user of gun bars, is not a hypocrite for critiquing rappers who use gun bars to seem tough or masculine; rather, he is challenging the style and framing of gun bars. For TDot rapping about guns in and of itself has no real relationship to masculinity. Rather, it is the way in which gun lyrics are styled and employed that speaks to a specific type of politic that is grounded in gendered performance.

Ironically, for Black men such as TDot, it was the way they queered gun lyrics that produced Black masculine sensibilities. Here, I am thinking in conversation with Evelynn Hammonds's contention that Black queer female sexualities are not just identities: "Rather, they represent discursive and material terrains where there exists the possibility for the active production of speech, desire, and agency."[39] To bend language, know desire, and strive for a piece of agency in a world hellbent on you not existing is queer. Dressing cars in drag and literally drag racing can be queer. Undergoing voice training to sing as a version of yourself that has been hidden from the world can be queer. All of it is the remaking of bodies so they can perform in ways that feel sincere. Guns lines are styled with imagery, metaphors, ad libs, and other poetic devices to remake the body of the lyric so that the listener can vibe to it. When Drop raps, "On one block they having church / The other block they loading bangers," he is using imagery to paint the complexity of the hood. When Paso raps, "I take my shot like they drafted me," he is using simile to show how hoop dreams often collide with the structural reality of the hood. It is dressing up the gun that makes the lyric powerful.

A tempered style of queer performativity has been used for cis Black men in the 252 to perform Black masculinity in humanizing ways. Something that feels like liberation will not be possible until there is a commitment to bodies that move and exist differently from theirs, though. Katherine McKittrick says that racism and sexism produce attendant geographies that are bound up in human disempowerment and dispossession.[40] If Black issues center Black men, and queer and feminist issues center white people, then Black women and queer-identifying people are positioned as placeless. If there is no place for Black queerness, then there is no space for Black masculinity to develop in ways that are honest to the beautiful, soft, and creative parts of who Black men are. This hurts.

CHAPTER 4

We Turned a Section 8 Apartment Into a Condo

Black folks in the 252 go out on Sundays. Most people do service or factory work, so their work schedule is unpredictable. The weekend is whatever day you have off that week. On Sunday nights folks from small towns across the 252 drive to Boat Ride in Rocky Mount. It has everything you want from a Black nightclub. Music that makes men wearing shirts that they paid too much money for wave stacks of twenty-dollar bills in the air. DJs that transition from songs about hustling to songs that have Black women singing at the top of their lungs about not taking their ex-man back. They play songs for men and women to meet in the middle of the dance floor under the red and blue strobe lights. The liquor softens the hardest parts of men, while giving women the courage to dance with a stranger as if love was made in the shadows of small buildings by two people whose bodies had the same choreography.

If we wanted to get out of the 252 on Sunday nights, we would go to one of the major cities surrounding the area code. In places like Raleigh, on nights that bars and clubs don't get as much foot traffic, they allow organizations to rent them out to host events that range from open mics to hip-hop showcases. This Sunday I pass on a night of drunk dancing at Boat Ride and head to James's place to watch him perform at a venue in Raleigh. James, twenty-seven years old, is a self-sufficient artist that has transformed one of his bedrooms into a one-stop shop for music production. He produces his own beats, engineers his own songs, and records them there.

"COORRREEEYYYYY," James screams as I walk through his front door.

"Jaaaammes," I yell back not as loud, but my voice carried enough to let him know that I tried to match his energy.

In a tone that is framed as joke, but not well enough to mask the seriousness and honesty within the statement, James says, "We ain't on that Black power shit tonight, we having fun." He is indicating that he doesn't want to hear about any Black social issues tonight.

"Alright, we good," I respond. I smile because that's what we do when we are together. We laugh, trash-talk, and live in moments that go on to live in our memory.

I understood why James didn't want me to be on my Black power shit when we went out that night. Most days he and the rest of the community encouraged me to offer an analysis of why something was the way it was. We turned talking about Black power shit into memories also. But folks didn't want to hear that when we were going out. Most of the week James was at work. Dealing with all the things working-class Black folk deal with at work. When he wasn't at work, he was living in a segregated neighborhood and helping keep a family together that is plagued with premature death. Losing adults young has a way of forcing everyone in the family to live a little older than they are. He was living Black power shit every day. This night and other nights we went out, James was attempting to live Blackness not bounded by the inequality that Black people face. He wanted to have a relational experience with me that exceeded the boundaries and limitations the South placed on Black people.

James was trying to teach me about placemaking. About how in the 252 we live with the ugliest of the South but are still southern and beautiful. Living in the carceral South does not mean you are bound by it. James felt this. He wanted me to do what Rebecca Louise Carter calls to "move beyond the boundaries of place altogether."[1] He believed that the way we related to each other that night could rework spatial and social boundaries to make the South feel like more than it was designed to be. We could change the vibe. This is not to deny or be momentarily blind to the assaults on Blackness but an investment in Black folks' ability to fracture geography and slip into pockets that feel like home.

We head to a hip-hop showcase in Raleigh where James is scheduled to perform to compete to win time on the local radio station, studio time to record a song, and marketing materials for a song. When we enter the venue, we walk down a long narrow hallway with brick walls to the left and right of us. It feels like we are walking into a basement. When you get to the end of the hallway the ceiling opens. There is a second level directly above you, where I imagine people stand and watch the small stage that is squeezed into the back right wall on the bottom floor.

It smells like beer. Boat Ride usually smells like eighty-dollar cologne masking weed smoke that seeps in from the outside area. On the wall left of the dance floor is the bar. Hanging tightly from the brick wall behind the bar are thirty rotating taps of craft beer. *We are not in the 252.* At Boat Ride beer comes either in a blue can or a clear bottle. There is no drink menu there. You say what you want, and if the bartender can make it, then it's available. But here there are drink specials and floating beer.

I realize if I am going to have fun at what I assumed was a white venue, then I need to try out one of the special drinks. There are only around fifteen people, just lingering. James goes and sits on a barstool in the back of the venue to mentally run through his set, and I head to the bar. I look at the floating beer and say, "Can I just get a whisky and coke."

I miss Boat Ride. There the bartenders were usually Black women dressed in a way that I'm sure brought in extra tips. I didn't want to seem broke around them. The service was slow there, because the bartenders danced and had conversations with their friends and family members between making drinks. These are friends who had Monday off, so they spent their Sunday night riding the boat.[2] I felt comfortable two-stepping there. I'm sure they have some version of Boat Ride in Raleigh. But I doubt that a place with floating beer could make me feel how Boat Ride does.

With my drink, James and I discuss his performance and his approach for tonight. I had no good advice, but he knew I would sing along and yell from the crowd. I'm a fan. People begin to filter into the open space in front of the stage. Around forty people. Enough to make the area near the stage dense, with walkable room in the rest of the venue. It was all Black people. Not just any Black people, but they smelled like my Black people from Boat Ride. As if they got in late because they had to smoke in the car before coming in.

"Y'all ready to hear some dope music?" the MC asks.

"Yeaaahhhh," I scream as my voice is drowned out by the collective scream of the audience. I love call-and-response. The way our voices can dance together without rehearsal. As if we hung out every weekend, like cousins or something.

"Let's give it up for Chris from the 252," the MC says as they introduce the first artist. Chris would go on to win the event. The crowd cheers to welcome Chris to the stage. He walks up on stage and the beat to his first song immediately comes on.

"I need everyone from the 252 to put your hands in air," he says. As I begin to raise my hand, I look around the room and see 70 percent of the crowd's hands go up. Maybe this is the 252. Instantly, Chris had connected with most of the audience. I don't remember Chris's first song. I do remember his vibe, though. The way he raised his hand simultaneously with the crowd and put up two fingers up, then five, then two. He made it feel like Boat Ride wasn't special because it was in the 252, but because the 252 was in Boat Ride. And the 252 is here now, in a bar with flying beer.

Chris was hype his whole set. Only 5'6", Chris felt big. He felt like an artist that we all knew. Someone we played in car rides and on Sunday nights. He danced and jumped around the stage signifying to the 252 continuously throughout his set. Chris had set the tempo for the entire night; he was in his bag.[3]

"So the 252 is in here deep tonight," the MC says.

The crowd would erupt so loud anytime someone made a 252 reference that it felt like the open space on the second level of the venue was filled with people. The 252 folks began to huddle up together in the audience once they began identifying each other. The long stretches of road between each of our towns now felt like they connected us more than separated us. Most of us had never met each other. But we made something in that moment that felt like community. It took me leaving the 252 to see that a hip-hop 252-identity not only existed but was a source of community and belonging for many artists. Even though there is competition and beef between many artists in the area, there is also love and care facilitated through the area code. The 252 is rural, poor, under-resourced, and policed heavily, but the identity comforts the insides of those from there. This is due to placemaking. The South is violent, but Black southerners find meaning through the crevice of light made possible by how they relate to each other. It is Black people's ability to make a white venue outside of the 252 feel like Boat Ride. Being Black in community with other Black people reshapes space, it moves where the South is and can be.

What is at stake here is in part a question of citizenship and belonging. Rinaldo Walcott contends that to be placed outside the category of citizen opens one up to routine and legal forms of violence from the state.[4] Walcott continues and argues, "Citizenship, then, is not really a measure of freedom, but rather a marker of what kinds or forms of abuse one might be subjected to."[5] Citizenship does not imply belonging. Black people in the 252 are legal citizens of the region but do not inherently belong there. Citizenship as a category is less about the rights of those with it and more about different modes of exclusion for those without it. Legal citizenship in a nation-state, in the words of Andrea A. Davis, does not take up differential access to affective, political, social, and cultural aspects of what it means to belong.[6] My point here is that Black people in the South have a legal claim to the region. However, Black people do not feel safe, loved, and protected in the South. The vibe is off.

The language of rights and legality often obscures the affective components that make up what it means to live in a place. Being legally American, southern, or anything else does not mean that those categories have made space for your fullness. What I learned from and with James that night is that it is the poetic and creative experience of being Black alongside other Black people that has forged a bond between Black people and the region. Region is mobile. We took the 252 to Raleigh. Regular Black folks in the 252 have fought less for ways to move toward a legal designation of citizen but rather have focused on creating moments that escape the physical and psychological violence of the South. In those moments, spaces, and creases, geography has mattered. Not because of space, though. It is the beauty, sound, and ideologies that are created in place that connects Black people to a larger Black diasporic spatial imaginary.

Geography matters because it is at what Murray Forman calls the "extreme local" that Black people have intimate encounters that allow them to develop belonging.[7] This belonging is not just to that locality but to a larger Black geography. Black folks across multiple Souths find meaning in the term "South" not because we share a similar southern experience but because all our divergent experiences tell us something about the multiple ways the South can show up and disadvantage Black people. We learn about what is done and what could be done to us through other Souths. Pain is not confined to borders. We push back against the South together. It is the way Black people love on each other, hold each other where they are, and reach out across borders that allows the South to feel like home. It is the affective work we do to change the vibe of the South that makes a Black South possible.

GOT SHOT AT, THEN DID TURKEY DRIVES ON THE SAME STREET

"Let's meet at Barnes & Noble," Oak says.

I haven't been to a bookstore since I been back to the 252. It's not that people in the 252 don't read, but most don't buy $30 books and overpriced coffee. Worn-out Bibles on end tables replace bookshelves in homes. My grandma thought it didn't matter how much you read if you didn't know the Word.[8] Besides the Bible, the Sunday paper is what holds folks' attention when they are consuming text. That's where rental homes, jobs, and coupons are. Reading in the 252 is about survival. It is about living better, something that some would believe can't be found in a place that sells $30 books and overpriced coffee.

Oak was born and raised in the 252 but had moved to Raleigh to pursue his art career. At twenty-five years old he is chasing his dream of acting, alongside rapping, painting, and dancing. Oak is creative. A large city like Raleigh provides more opportunities for him to find work centered on the breadth of his talents. He has long, black, coarse hair, and people often call him "Black Jesus." He lives like Jesus too. Oak can go to the hood in the 252 and get along with everyone, or he could just as easily sit in a place that sells overpriced coffee and be comfortable. There was always more to him than what his tight-legged pants and jean jackets showed.

Oak is waiting for me at a small table by the coffee shop. As I sit we greet each other and try to find common ground to build our conversation on. That verbal dance you do when you haven't spoken to someone in a while.

"I just been working. Taking it easy," I say, responding to Oak asking how I been. In the 252 we are similar. We are part of the few who went off to university. Neither of us ever really knew we were 252 until we left there. I think we saw that in each other. That no matter how much we cosplayed at Black middle-classness, no matter how many expensive coffees we could afford or meetings we had at bookstores, there was still rural poverty inside of us. For us to connect, that was the ground we had to meet each other at. For this conversation to feel honest, something would have to be said about how where we came from moved with us. We would have to go back to the 252.

We begin to talk about what it is like for him to have a job in Raleigh.

"Every day I step out, I feel like I'm on the battlefield. Even at my job. At my little dinky job where it's a bunch of white folks smiling all the time. Folks may see me in pictures with them and think I live a good life. They may even have a lot of stereotypical thoughts of me. Like that nigga a sellout. But it still feels like a battlefield," Oak says.

"I know what you mean," I respond. I do. I know what it feels like to have pictures posted of me on social media, and family back home see me diversifying the workplace. Pictures showing that I broke through the boundaries of my segregated town and have gotten close enough to white folks that they don't mind standing shoulder to shoulder with me. But behind the phone screen. Behind the work-appropriate clothes. Behind my Black skin, even past my flesh. Somewhere around my core, I feel what Oak is saying.

"Regardless of where we at, they still have to treat us all like criminals," Oak says.

As we sit at a small table that could accommodate only two cups of coffee, he tells me about a time he was walking to the local corner store and was approached by officers. After indicating that he was just going to the store, they detained him by placing cuffs on his wrists and laying him down. While he physically survived the encounter, his relationship to the street that he walked was changed. When you are slammed to the ground, your face learns things about the sidewalk that your feet take for granted. The sidewalk has a smell, taste, and texture. When you spend your whole life stepping on something, it is difficult to see how it has qualities like yours. Maybe that's why the cops needed Oak on the ground.

If the cops would have stood and talked with Oak, maybe the smell of the castor oil in his hair would have reminded them of summers they spent in nature. Maybe listening to why he was going to the corner store would have reminded them of the taste of twenty-five-cent candy that as a kid was always sweeter when you paid for it yourself. Maybe if they listened and didn't touch him, they could have felt him in a different way. Understood that he had qualities similar to theirs. None of this was possible with him beneath them. I felt low listening to Oak tell this story. His voice trembled when he recalled what had been done to him. During that encounter he was let go and wasn't physically harmed. But it was the possibility of violence, the feeling that your body is not really your body because it is at the mercy of someone of who doesn't understand its curves or mannerisms.

This happened at home. On the streets we walk daily. On the streets that connect all the spaces, places, and people that make the 252 possible. These streets hold trauma. In understanding Oak's experience, I want to think with James Baldwin. In Baldwin's famous 1969 Dick Cavett interview when discussing the police, he says:

> And no matter how many people say, "You're being paranoid when you talk about police brutality"—I know what I'm talking about. I survived those streets and those precinct basements and I know. And I'll tell you this—I know what it was like when I was really helpless, how many beatings I got. And I know what happens now because I'm not really helpless. But I know, too, that if he [police] don't know that this is Jimmy Baldwin and not just some other nigger he's gonna blow my head off just like he blows off everybody else's head. It could happen to my mother in the morning, to my sister, to my brother. . . . For me this has always been a violent country.[9]

For Baldwin it is the lived and felt experience of Blackness that Black people understand who they are to this country. To Baldwin the feeling of helplessness encapsulates what it means to move as a Black person. For folks like

Oak, getting a nice job and moving out of the 252 did not shake this feeling. The South is mobile. What I mean by this is that Oak's body may not still feel the physical pain of that encounter, but it remembers the sound of the soundwalk. It is in moments of survival that we learn about what a place is to us. Those lessons are what fill the empty spaces inside us, give us shape.

Legal texts such as birth certificates and apartment leases give Black people legal claim to the 252. But anti-Blackness perpetuated through a carceral system shapes the texture and context of the South, positioning the Black community outside the ontological bounds of belonging. To say this differently, Black people in the 252 have official documentation stating that they belong to this region, but they do not feel that they can live, move, and breathe honestly here. Being bestowed legal rights gave a form of circumscribed citizenship. It did not make Black sound, feeling, and movement acceptable ways of being. Saidiya Hartman showed that discourse on rights and self-possessed individualism helped transition Black people to different modes of oppression.[10] As people with rights and self-determination, Black people now become the bearers of responsibility for their condition. To police and criminalize someone, they must first have the legal ability to make choices. The criminalization of Blackness depended on them having legal rights. The South's large-scale ideological and cultural investment in punishment and criminalization produces Black subjects within/without prison walls as warranting containment in ways that do not challenge their legal designation as free.

This shows up in the music. The feeling of helplessness. The feeling of home being violent. Knowing that legal rights do not keep the softest parts of you safe when Black people have been made to be the hardest problem to fix in the South. This is why Oak raps, paints, acts, and dances. He wants to get to the non-wordness of Black life.

"If I could put everything into words, then I wouldn't have got into painting and all the other artforms," Oak says.

We feel much more of the contradictions of home than is sayable. Art gets us closer to communicating the vibe of space. The way home is complicated. Home is not necessarily the safest place but the place that struggling with its contradictions allows you to better understand yourself.

SOUNDING HOME

I have had a gun pointed at me or ridden around with one only in places that I stayed long enough to call home. Statistically this is probably the case because the more time you spend in any one place, the more opportunities there are for violence. There is also an intimacy to violence. When people get too close to anything I really care about, that is when my defenses come up. That is more possible at home. When we weren't ad-libbing songs together, Drop and I talked about home. Largely about what it meant to be brought to stolen land and work out your relationship to that place. About how white folks owned everything, even the run-down neighborhoods they wouldn't live in. They were still the ones who made money from them. This led us to think about all the unruly things we did to convince ourselves that someplace, even if it's only a street, could be ours.

"When I outgrew the reckless stuff, I realized we are fighting over turf," Drop tells me while sitting directly in from of me in this empty restaurant. Looking at me as if he were confessing. "Shooting over turf, but we don't own none of this. None of this land or property we own. It's landing us dead or in prison. This our neighborhood, though, even though it don't really belong to us."

I think, but don't say it, that society thinks those Black men who do violence in their neighborhoods are the reason they are dangerous. They think if we all just hugged each other and loved better through the poverty, underfunded schools, and too few resources, then we could have a neighborhood that was safe to call home. Or a home that was safe. I didn't have to say it, Drop and I both already knew what the US thought of us. Drop wanted me to know that home is complicated. It may not be safe, ours to own, or filled with people who know how to make the most out of bad options. But it is home. I too have wanted to be reckless in the town I call home, when a nigga stole my mother's car stereo. The quietness in her ride to work reminded her that anything could be taken from her in our neighborhood, even the staticky radio stations that barely made it out to the country. I wanted parts of my community to hurt like I did.

"I love my hood. Don't get me wrong," Drop says as he puts his critiques into perspective. He was honest. That despite the despair in the rural Black South, Black people build structures of relatedness that reshape how space is embodied, lived, and understood. Here there are no big skylines to block the community's vision of when and where the sun is shining. They can see brightness in moments that may be shaded in other spaces. It is often grappling with, naming, and embracing the despair that forges bonds within the community. That allows us to see the bright spots. Drop and I did this through pain music. The sharing, singing, and talking about songs that made space for all the things we felt but wished we didn't have to.

Making space for Black people in the South has often come from (re)sounding the South. By this I mean moments we create new or attend to the often-unheard frequencies of the region. Listening to the desperation in actions and hearing beyond what American logics would tell us. After Mook stole my mother's stereo, I eventually learned a different way of listening to the stomach growl of a high school student who had little family support and was desperate for cash. I could hear the shame in his scalp when he looked at the floor and scratched his head whenever I saw him after. Mook was responding to a version of the South he was forced to survive in. His body said this. I stopped hating him when I realized we were living a similar song. This is the work pain music attempts to do. It takes us to those moments of violence, which most often occur at home, and forces us to sit within it and hear the often-unsayable pieces of rural Black life in the South. If we can hear and feel otherwise, then we can have a better understanding of where the South is. It's not as far from the Old South as we would like to assume.

To tell an honest story about home, I had to go back to mine. To Weldon. Where Sabrina worked so hard to get Jon out of. Where Amp was murdered. Where my mother planted a garden. All these stories dealt with pieces of the terribleness that the South reserved for poor rural Black people. They show the multiple ways we attempt to survive concentrated poverty and how sometimes we don't. They also offer glimpses of something more. They show community members working to validate the softest and hardest parts of people who live fast. Even that type of life is motivated by an understanding of how structural forces steal time from Black people. They show people making beauty. Whether it is shirts with the faces of lost loved ones on them or flowers that were not afraid to grow up in the projects. Sonically, the closest I feel to the complexness of home is Mane's album *Live from Hurley Ave 3.*[11] Hurley Ave is in Weldon, but it is not simply Weldon. It is gritty and vulnerable. It is loud and has whispers of calm. *Live from Hurley Ave 3* recasts how I hear home and how the 252 is understood and embodied.

I be posted on Hurley Ave,
Cuz I'm out here trying to go get this cash.
And I don't scream Roanoke Rapids, South Weldon, or Halifax,
B*tch I'm from Scoco Park,
—Fukk Da World, Mane

The lyrics above are from a single Mane released in anticipation of his latest album entitled *Live from Hurley Ave 3*. The song has a relaxed beat, and the lyrics take center stage. Also, to divert the listener to the lyrics, the song is structured as a freestyle and has no chorus. Hurley Ave is the street Mane grew up on in a neighborhood called Scoco Park. There is no playground in Scoco Park. No trees to protect you from the southern heat. There has recently been a basketball court built there. One rim is broken, so after shots, kids clear the ball at the three-point line, never getting to feel what's it's like to run with all their might in the park. To be able to move beyond spaces where shots can happen at.

Mane did three installments of *Live from Hurley Ave*, and as I write this, he is working on the fourth. There is something about being a southern, 252, or a Weldon rapper that didn't do his insides justice. There are things that only the street he lived his entire life on knew about him. Before we could feel him, we had to hear the stillness of the mobile homes on his street. We had to hear the way the grass there struggled to grow and always ended up patchy. This single does this work by creating conceptual distance not only from neighboring cities but also from Weldon. He distances himself from the other side of Weldon, which is walking distance from his neighborhood. The conceptual distance matters in ways that space can't account for. There are hierarchies within the 252. Even with the area code's median household income well below the national average, Scoco Park is understood to be one of the poorest neighborhoods in the area. Most people from that street would say they are from Weldon or the 252 depending on who is asking and their familiarity with the area. But for Mane, hip-hop demanded a more honest accounting of where he is from. His pain and all his intimate faculties are tied to his street. That's where "Fukk Da World" takes us. The daily life, the lost life, and imagined life of what it means to live on Hurley Avenue.

Mane has said that his street is his inspiration. It is not that he takes his life and puts it in a song, but rather there is a reciprocal relationship between his street and pain music. Experiences are not static. Sitting within the most difficult moments of living on Hurley Ave and trying to communicate them reshapes how he knows his home. Hip-hop became localized in Hurley Ave by restructuring local languages, providing a space to rethink desires, and constructed an identity that is constantly in motion. It is not that the song mimics how Hurley Ave sounds, but rather it allows us to hear the street in a new way. It changes the vibe of Weldon. By this I mean that it allows us to have different memories and bodily experiences in that space. We can feel it in a new way.

Mane didn't identify specifically with the 252 or his city, but with his street because hip-hop provided an avenue to create specific modes of identification. When creating his rap lyrics and videos, he made a series of choices and constructed an understanding of himself that only his street was nuanced enough to capture. Hurley Ave being socially constructed as one of the worst parts of the 252, Mane had another layer of exclusion and marginalization to deal with. Articulating a struggle specific to his street has allowed him and others the ability to engage with notions of belonging to what Forman calls the "extreme local."[12] Forman suggests that rappers draw inspiration not only from regional affiliation but from streets, telephone area codes, and other specific sociospatial information. While drawing inspiration from the extreme local, artists simultaneously restructure and recast the conceptual bounds of the 252.

Mane is part of the 252 because he is from Hurley Ave. His belonging to the 252 is a consequence of his innermost self being tied to a street that sits in the area code. He is southern not because he has an allegiance to a monolithic South but because the most intimate capacities of his body are dedicated to Hurley Ave, which sits within the South. Similarly, African Americans are American not because of a search for an ideal type of citizenship in the US but because they are committed to the Black folks who sit next to them, and that demands grappling with what it means to live in this country. The point here is that our commitments and desires are aimed at what is close to us, but our attentiveness to those things closest to our inner selves demand a recognition and engagement with larger spaces and systems that shape where we are.

This recasting of the extreme local is not simply a cultural or social phenomenon but a political negotiation. It is making the 252 legible within oneself and the broader political climate. Political communication does not exist independent from the same kind of considerations that determine our responses to aesthetic and cultural stimuli.[13] Music shapes how we hear and where we listen in a range of aspects of our life. For Mane and others, these songs are not experienced as secondary to how broader society understands Hurley Ave, but rather these songs are part of what it means to live and embody Hurley Ave. As the South moves, these songs are part of that push-and-pull.

It is the way Black people move, make sounds, and be still in places that makes that space what it is to them. The broader carceral organization of the South places limits on how Black people in the region live, but it is through the way Black people relate to each other that the South develops new possibilities. Black people are just as historically, emotionally, and socially important to the South as the limited vision that white people had for it. Recasting Hurley Ave through hip-hop is not seen as using art to make political statements, but it is political, because embodying the area code produces new modes of being here. Just as mainstream political discourse aims to set forth a vision for specific geographical spaces, so does pain music. It uses those inner pieces of Black life to revise the South. This is placemaking.

This is what Oak was expressing at the bookstore.

"I want to be a newspaper for our rural areas and to articulate a message that our reverends and pastors can't because of their reach. I needed as many tools as possible to reach the community," Oak tells me. The Black performative space offers the community a resource not given by mainstream institutions.

In elaborating on what makes this possible, Oak says, "Hip-hop is freeing. You need approval to engage in biology. You must meet certain requirements to be a chemist, but when you are in the arts you don't even need a school. It gives the community the ability to tell their story without being constrained."

Oak teaches the arts to help make extra money, and he is not suggesting that there are not formal skills, technologies, and sensibilities that need to be learned prior to becoming an artist. He is contending that there are not as many systemic limitations to developing this knowledge base. Art is not as weighed down by the carceral logics of the South as much as other areas. If there is a possibility to remember, know, and engage the South in ways not overly determined by what white people set the region out to be, pain music is that possibility. The anger, fear, despair, and commitment not to conform to the respectable allows for sounds to be conceived that are foreclosed by nonstigmatized emotions. Pain music challenges how citizenship is popularly perceived. *Fuck the world.* It shows the South in a new light that is not contained by rigid boundaries that would make us believe that a knowable South is possible. Breaking away from the good, respectable, knowable, and palatable offers us an opportunity to engage with pieces of the South that have been hidden from history and maps. The unruly parts that don't conform to positivist ways of knowing.

The guns, drugs, and fucks in southern hip-hop are popularity interpreted as part of Black people's negligence.[14] This is part of a larger history of dehumanizing and criminalizing Black people to resolve the contradictions of the country. If Black people were seen as a version of human that had thinking and feeling capabilities, then we would have to make sense of why people who love gently and think deeply would be attracted to such dark sounds. This would make us have to grapple with what has been done to Black people. Locate where all this heaviness came from. To protect the reputation of the country, we criminalize the trap sound and obscure the skill, methods, and emotions that go into making Black life audible.

The *Live from Hurley Ave* series produced an alternative archive of the street. This does not imply that these albums tell the most accurate narrative of the street, but it pushes back one-dimensional readings of place. It highlights the rickety bridge between what is done to a place and how people live there. That space is shaky and contested. The albums are a rendering of the unseen, not solely to the listener but to the artists themselves. Writing about a place will impact how we know and experience it. It gives the place a new texture, a different vibe.

Our birth certificates provide text that gives us claim to the South. There is more to lived experience and music than the text, though. The context in which Black people exist in the South is in a state of precarity and vulnerability. Through (re)sounding the South, Black people have changed the vibe of the region. They have listened for and produced frequencies that push against exclusionary notions of citizenship and developed relationships that are grounded in reciprocal ways of living better together. These relationships are why we love Hurley Ave. Black people in the 252 have worked to make the South, even if just a street, feel like home despite all the violence.

OUR HEART, OUR HOME

Even when every legal document you own says you are from a place, that alone can't convince your flesh not to hide between your skin and bones if it feels you can't live freely there. Those documents don't make you want to open up to an area when the vibe is off. Black people in the 252 love the area code but dream of it being somewhere else. They want the 252 to be somewhere that Black skin doesn't feel like a prison. They want it to be where we can have honest conversations about our memories and how to collectively live better. This is what Saidiya Hartman meant when she said that "desire is as reliable as any map."[15] Our longings and yearnings tell us something about where we are at and where we need to get to. The goal of a map is to create boundaries, borders, and separation. This rigidness obscures how space is felt and experienced.

Belonging to a place is less about ownership than about how you exist in relation to what's central to that community. The people, the red dirt, the rivers, and everything else that makes a place possible. On my return to the 252, I was a new version of myself. My southern drawl had been compromised by living in Baltimore and listening to podcasts where people take too many dramatic pauses to say nondramatic things. I now dressed how I imagined those people who take dramatic pauses dressed. A messenger bag and a too-tight collared shirt. But I style mine with Jordans. I'm comfortable this way.

Early in my return, I went to a soul food buffet. I had a friend visiting and I wanted to take them to a place to taste the town. All the fried chicken and fish one could want. This Carolina BBQ wasn't here before I left. It was on the other side of town in a small dark building. This building didn't aesthetically look much different, though. The only thing that really changed was that this is a better location near the highway, and the prices had gone up. The server walks us to our seats, getting a small pad out to take our drink orders.

"Where y'all from?" the server asks, glancing simultaneously at both of us. Inviting either of us to answer.

"I'm from here," I say. My voice didn't cup the air the way his did, though. I didn't sound 252 when I said it.

"Who yo people?" he asks. The ask was polite. We probably knew somebody or of somebody that was connected to each other. We were building a piece of rapport that would make our next hour together kinder and softer.

"Who yo people" is a geographical question. It is about where your commitments reside and where you forge community. The server could have easily asked me what part of the 252 I was from when I indicated that I am from the area. But being from an area is not about ownership of physical space, but rather about reciprocal relationships with the people and touchstones that make a place a place. The sound of the 252 isn't just in how we pronounce our syllables, but in the ways we articulate life in the space we imagine to be the 252. The sound of the area code is in the quiet of community members who sleep at 2:00 p.m. because they work third shift at the food packaging plant. It is in the humming of your uncle fixing cars in the summer heat in his backyard so he can stay home and watch the kids while your mother is at work. The sound of the 252 is all the auditory frequencies that make up Black living in the area code.

For Black people in the South, belonging has not been about blindly accepting American legal and juridical understandings of space. To be of and from a place is about being invested in the relational processes that continuously revise where a place is at. What it means to be American and southern in the traditional sense has always relied on some form of exclusion of Black people. Black southerners have worked to un/map the South. They have pushed back against the boundaries of exclusion and rigidness of the South that makes mapping possible. They have done this through resounding and changing the vibe of the South to accommodate them. Mainstream institutions in many ways have not allowed Black people in the South and beyond to forge belonging in sincere ways. Pain music is one instance of (re)sounding the South so we can better hear where the South is at.

Kris is an artist from Kinston who recently received a bachelor's degree in history. Kris is like me in that we both thought college would allow us to know our home better or at least differently. We are both trying to (re)sound the 252 but struggle with questions around sincerity, since neither one of us live there permanently. When discussing his goals and purpose for his music, Kris's responses tended to be directed at recalibrating his relationship to his hometown.

"Of course, it would be nice to have a nice car that I bought with money from my music. Those things are nice, and I'm not saying they are outside the goal, but at the same time I would say the ultimate goal is to influence how people remember me and my city," Kris says.

People often bring "good" answers to interviews. Even I attempted to bring a well-packaged version of who I am. To push Kris in his answer, I ask, "What do you mean by influence memory?"

"For instance, those hurricanes that recently hit. North Carolina didn't provide any relief to my neighborhood. The Black community, we supported each other. Some folks had a clothing line, aunties were selling plates, we made it possible for the city to move forward. That's what people need to know."

I cite Kris here briefly to make a larger point about placemaking. That placemaking is less about mapped-out spaces and more about relational processes that make living better possible. Kris had to move out of the 252 because he struggled to find work there. He did not stop contributing to the cultural production of the 252 though. Even outside of the geographical boundaries of how to 252 is popularly mapped, Kris does what Marcus Hunter refers to as using everyday Black wisdom to recalibrate how cities are remembered by providing alternative historical timelines in the face of mainstream white evocation.[16] Black storytelling offers a way forward to the past. This does not get Black people out of the structural context in which they exist. Rather, it changes the texture of how we remember the South.

I want to say that home is in the song. I don't know if it's corny, and it doesn't quite get to the point I'm trying to make. I'm trying to say something like Baldwin's prose: "We had the liquor, the chicken, the music, and each other, and had no need to pretend to be what we were not." For Baldwin something that felt like freedom was in reach, not in the retreat from the very real conditions in which Black people contend but through the ways he survived them in community. It wasn't about creating a place without the ugliness but about the moments we were honest about the ugliness and the corners of our mouths still found ways to turn up to catch a smile. For

Baldwin, songs that chronicle the pain and suffering of Black experience are not inherently sad songs, but rather they are freeing in the way they allow Black people to live, or what he calls "to be present in all that one does."[17] Pain music is allowing Black people in the 252 to develop belonging not in the ways it has allowed them to escape the structural positioning of Blackness but through allowing them to bring their full selves to bear in the face of whatever they may have to contend with. It is not the songs in and of themselves that do this work, but rather the process of using one's emotional subjectivity to archive the South and experiencing these songs in community with those who understand the depths out of which such a tenacity comes. Liberation is not a goal but a process; Black southerners along the journey have creatively remade their relationship to the South—they have pursued the emotional benefits of belonging that the Western notion of citizenship may not be capable of offering.

Lately I been drinking out the bottle,
I ain't been getting no sleep,
Riding round the city just thinking,
Thinking how I gone bring back Pee,
—G50, "Sleep"[18]

Closing Verse

I don't have to drive tonight. Usually, I'm the one driving to events. Tonight I can be as reckless as I want. I feel like I did when I was a teenager getting dropped off on the other side of town with only ten dollars to my name and faith that I will see someone that night who will give me a ride home. This is faith in my relationship to place: that despite the little I have, when I am in my own town, everything will always work itself out. I have that type of hope for tonight. Jeff is going to drive me and two of his friends forty minutes to Virginia for a party.

Being released from driving, I decided to pregame and have a few drinks before we headed out. Three drinks would be enough to make the car ride feel quicker and leave me with room to have another drink once we got there. As we are in Jeff's home preparing, his friends begin rolling up.[1] I smoke only on special occasions. Tonight is an occasion. For the next hour, we talk over music and through the smoke that is between us. We enjoy the moment.

As Jeff is driving, I watch the woods that sits on both sides of the road, checking to see if any deer are lurking. It's late, so I know everything that moves in the 252 is looking for a safe passage to somewhere. While I search for wildlife, the grass lights up. I turn and see cop lights behind us. While Jeff decelerates there is a quiet in the car, as if we assume the cop can hear us from his vehicle.

"Where are you heading to speeding?" the cop asks. Loaded question.

"We going out for the night," Jeff says. The officer responds and I can't catch what he is saying, but I hear the word "marijuana." Jeff says he hasn't been smoking, which he hasn't. The officer asks us four Black boys to get out the car and stand on the side of the road beside a tobacco field in the dead of night. I am nervous, not because we have marijuana but because we are Black boys and marijuana could be his excuse to treat us like Black boys. This white officer standing at around 5'10" looks at us and says if we give him the marijuana and the cash we have, he will let us go.

"I only have forty dollars," I say. That was more honest than it should have been. I didn't feel like I owned anything else I carried in that moment. All of it was at his mercy.

Collectively we give the officer around 140 bucks and forty dollars' worth of weed. I felt the terribleness that comes with home. A white rural southerner looking for some sense of meaning in the unfulfilled promises of power. I left that moment with uncertainty. I did not know if Jeff was speeding. I did not know if we were stopped because we were Black. I do not know how differently the officer would have responded stopping four white women smelling like weed. Katherine McKittrick in *Dear Science* points to the way a story "cannot tell itself without our willingness to imagine what it cannot tell."[2] That night has sat in my mind, not because it better helped me understand race and its relationship to the South but because it forced me to grapple with what it means not to know. To feel so much and be unsure about just as much.

I returned home to the 252 to try to learn *something* about where I came from, hoping I would figure out why I sound the way I do. Why don't I sound like Black people across the ocean? Why my mama sometimes say I talk like white folks, when she the one who wanted me to be taught by them? What I am saying is that I don't remember who my folks were before they came to America, and I often forget how to curve my vowels how my mama curves hers, since I spent so much of my adult life around white folks. What the South does is demand you to forget what your people sound like if you want to have any semblance of stability. When they can't use the breadth of an ocean to keep distance between us and our past, they tell us stories that don't demonstrate what they exactly did to our mamas and aunties. Part of being southern and Black is not knowing who we were before we were southern and Black. I'm coming to grips with the idea that this memory will forever be stolen from me. That I will never know. Even without the memory I still feel that connection. The same way my insides tell me that there is something before the South, it tells me there is something about the way white folks talk about my mama and her choices that just doesn't sound right. Regardless of ever finding those more honest stories, I returned home because I needed to hear and feel where I came from. If there was so much about my existence that I would never know, I wanted to at least get closer to those feelings that let me know I am missing something inside of me.

I let go of the idea of the quantifiable and wanted to explore what the softest parts of some of the hardest niggas I know could tell me about where the South was. I wanted to say something honest about where I came from and about how that honesty could let us know the South better. To me, the hustlers and trappers were honest. They leaned into their desires. They attempted to actualize the unfulfilled promises of America. They were also the ones who usually felt the worst of the South. They experienced death fast. They became entangled with officers as both believed their freedom was dependent upon the abolition of the other.

It was through vibing with them that I felt the 252. Standing shoulder to shoulder with them in front of police officers and at vigils. Rapping along with them and laughing at how my voice struggled to find the beat. Hearing the way their voice lost bass when they spoke to their mothers. These moments gave me glimpses of their commitments. They signified where they were trying to go. To know where you want to go, you must have some inkling of where you are at. They were in the South.

For me the South is home. It was in the words of Toni Morrison that I found my way back. The care that Paul D and Sethe, two former slaves, had for each other helped move me closer to the South. Paul D says to Sethe:

> I'm not saying this because I need a place to stay. That's the last thing I need. I told you, I'm a walking man, but I been heading in this direction for seven years. Walking all around this place. Upstate, downstate, east, west; I been in territory ain't got no name, never staying nowhere long. But when I got here and sat out there on the porch, waiting for you, well, I knew it wasn't the place I was heading toward; it was you.[3]

The lines on maps don't make a space. They divide it. Rather it is the relational experiences of people who sit on porches that build a place. Cartography is a way of being. The South is not a singular geographical space, but rather the name we give to the social formations that happen in a specific region. Black people have lived in community and developed relations. South is a way to name where these relations are happening. We have related across borders. The South is mobile. I looked for the South inside of women and men that America tried to convince me were the problem with the region. Inside of people abused by the region but committed to preventing others from bleeding like them. They taught me that to look for the South is not to look for a place but to look for the people who make something that we call South possible. This is what I heard and felt in the 252. People making something possible.

ACKNOWLEDGMENTS

In one way I always knew this book was possible. Maybe not necessarily in this format. But I knew that the way I lived and put words together would help direct someone to the South. In another way I didn't think that I would ever write this text. I didn't think I could sit long enough in the pain. I didn't think my voice could hold the story. I didn't think I could say what my body knew.

This is a thank-you to those who helped me learn how to sit in the pain without it consuming me. They usually did this by sitting in it with me. I want to thank those who taught me that it is not my voice's job to carry the story of the South. Rather, my voice must speak in a way that would compel the South to speak back to me. It would be in that conversation that we can hear the South. I want to thank those who taught me to trust my body. To listen to what my fingertips, knees, and thin hairs on my arm are saying. I had to learn my body in a new way.

To thank anybody, first I would have to thank my mama. Thank you for being a Black mama. Thank you for breathing. When you stopped, it hurt. I'm not sure if I can remember how to be the version of happy that I was when you were alive. You breathed for me. I'm going to try to do the same for others.

To Karizma. Thank you for trusting me to be your big brother. For giving me an opportunity to do right by you, even when I may not have deserved the way you love. To Wink. I want to be strong like you. You held our family up. You make home possible. To Elijah. You were my first best friend. You taught me how to care about those who are close to you. I needed that for this book.

To the 252. The people who shared their inner lives with me. To the trees, dirt, and rivers. To everything and everyone not afraid to live there. Thank you for being 252.

To Kwame. You are kind and gentle. You saw a scholar in me when I didn't. I'm still trying to convince myself to trust your judgment about me the same way I trust it about everything else. Thank you.

To my grandma. You read the Bible every morning. White folks think bookshelves, bookstores, and coffee shops communicate something about one's commitment to reading. Don't none of that matter if you don't know the Word.

To the scholars who loved on me and dared me to write this in my own voice. To B. Brian Foster. Thank you for teaching me that sentences can be beautiful. To Regina Bradley. Thank you for giving me the courage to write without thinking about white folks. To Nghana Lewis. Thank you for saying what needed to be said, so I could write what needed to be written.

To the gang. Que, Mike, and Malcolm. We really out here in these streets doing the thang. Thank y'all for loving me, no matter what stage of life I am in.

To my academic squad. Theresa, Devon, Jennifer, Pyar, Patrice, Rahsaan, and Brittany. Y'all inspire me to think more honestly. Thank you.

To institutions that supported this project. Morgan State University and Virginia Tech are where I learned how to struggle with ideas. Augustana College, American Sociological Association Minority Fellowship Program Cohort 45, and Tulane University's Deans and Provost Office all invested in me financially to give me the space and privilege to think.

Dr. Brunsma. Dr. Faulkner. Dr. Copeland. Y'all read the ugliest version of this book and believed that I could turn it into something the world would want to see. Thank you.

Writing this is hard.

There are so many names that deserve to be mentioned but will not be. I would not feel comfortable if I did not thank every artist, athlete, and hustler from the 252 daring to dream of a new world. Daring to take what was denied them. Daring to hope. Hope is a practice. It is doing the work even when your circumstances make it unlikely that you will get what you deserve.

To Kiese Laymon, Imani Perry, and Jesmyn Ward. I have never met y'all. But I don't believe I would know myself without reading y'all. Thank you for writing the South.

To everyone I have spoken with, laughed with, argued with, tweeted with, waved at, and exchanged head nods with in the past six years. Those small moments taken together make up life. Those are the moments that made this book possible. Thank you.

To anyone who loved me enough to read this book, thank you.

NOTES

INTRODUCTION: THE 2–5–2

1. Their acknowledgment that I could thrive in the white world did not make them read me as white, but it was assumed that I was positioned closer to the privileges and the over criticalness of whiteness.

2. Imani Perry, *South to America: A Journey below the Mason-Dixon to Understand the Soul of a Nation* (New York: Ecco, 2022), xvi.

3. "Unfeeling" refers to the work of Xine Yao. Thinking about how Black people feel otherwise or choose not to feel anything. Xine Yao, *Disaffected: The Cultural Politics of Unfeeling in Nineteenth-Century America* (Durham, NC: Duke University Press, 2021).

4. Rebecca Louise Carter, "Valued Lives in Violent Places: Black Urban Placemaking at a Civil Rights Memorial in New Orleans," *City & Society* 26, no. 2 (2014): 239–61.

5. Corey Miles, "Black Rural Feminist Trap: Stylized and Gendered Performativity in Trap Music," *Journal of Hip Hop Studies* 7, no. 1 (2020): 45–46.

6. McKittrick, Katherine, "Mathematics Black Life," *Black Scholar* 44, no. 2 (2014): 17.

7. Vibe is often a method of accounting that escapes the rigidness of formal and disciplinary language. Given vibe pushes back against making the world static, I search for multiple ways to explain vibe, rather than having one static definition.

8. My use of "South" is a reference to the US South. I say "South" intentionally, as it operates as a frame for understanding not only geographically but racially and culturally in the American imagery.

9. Zora Neale Hurston, "How It Feels to Be Colored Me," in *I Love Myself When I Am Laughing . . . and Then Again When I Am Looking Mean and Impressive: A Zora Neale Hurston Reader*, ed. Alice Walker (New York: Feminist Press at the CUNY, 1979), 154.

10. W. E. B. Du Bois, *The Souls of Black Folks* (New York: Bantam, originally published in 1903 [1989]): 1–2.

11. Kiese Laymon, *Heavy: An American Memoir* (New York: Simon and Schuster, 2018), 9.

12. A. Bennett, "41 Percent of NC Towns Are Declining in Population: The Worst Are in the Northeast," *Newsobserver*, July 6, 2017, https://www.newsobserver.com/news/local/article159740514.html.

13. Saidiya Hartman, *Lose Your Mother: A Journey along the Atlantic Slave Route* (New York: Farrar, Straus and Giroux, 2007), 6.

14. I am using a conception of placemaking from Marcus Anthony Hunter, Mary Pattillo, Zandria F. Robinson, and Keeanga-Yamahtta Taylor, "Black Placemaking: Celebration, Play, and Poetry," *Theory, Culture & Society* 33, no. 7–8 (2016): 31.

15. Harin Contractor and Spencer Overton, "An Introduction to the Future of Work in the Black Rural South," Joint Center for Political and Economic Studies (2020): 6.

16. Eddie Glaude Jr., *Begin Again: James Baldwin's America and Its Urgent Lessons for Our Own* (New York: Crown, 2020), 43.

17. Katherine McKittrick, *Dear Science and Other Stories* (Durham, NC: Duke University Press, 2020), 7.

18. Faith Kurtyka, "Trends, Vibes, and Energies: Building on Students' Strengths in Visual Composing," *Across the Disciplines: A Journal of Language, Learning, and Academic Writing* 12, no. 4 (2015), http://wac.colostate.edu/atd/performing_arts/kurtyka2015.cfm; Andrew Friedman, "Mårten Spångberg and the Vibe of Contemporaneity," *Theater* 44, no. 3 (2014): 8, https://doi.org/10.1215/01610775-2714538.

19. Eduardo Bonilla-Silva, "Feeling Race: Theorizing the Racial Economy of Emotions," *American Sociological Review* 84, no. 1 (2019): 2, https://jps.library.utoronto.ca/index.php/des/article/view/22168.

20. Shantara Nicole Strickland, "For the Sake of Freedom: Landownership, Education, and Memory in Halifax County, North Carolina, 1900–1960," MA thesis, North Carolina State University, 2012, 91, https://repository.lib.ncsu.edu/handle/1840.16/8295.

21. Alopecia is a medical condition that impacts the hair follicles, causing mild to extreme hair loss.

22. John M. Eason, *Big House on the Prairie: Rise of the Rural Ghetto and Prison Proliferation* (Chicago: University of Chicago Press, 2017), 40.

23. "Greenville, NC Crime," Areavibes, https://www.areavibes.com/greenville-nc/crime/

24. Policing in the South emerged from slave patrols. Mariame Kaba goes into this history and the potential future of policing in Mariame Kaba. *We Do This' til We Free Us: Abolitionist Organizing and Transforming Justice* (Chicago: Haymarket Books, 2021), 14.

25. Jennifer Tilton. "Race, Rage and Emotional Suspects: Ideologies of Social Mobility Confront the Racial Contours of Mass Incarceration," *Children & Society* 34, no. 4 (2020): 291–304.

26. James Baldwin, *The Fire Next Time* (New York: Dial Press, 1963), 26.

27. Data on Black women's and girls' rate of incarceration can be found at: The Sentencing Project, "Incarcerated Women and Girls," Sentencing Project, November 6, 2019, https://www.sentencingproject.org/publications/incarcerated-women-and-girls/; and Lauren Camera, "Black Girls Are Twice as Likely to Be Suspended, in Every State," *US News*, May 9, 2017, https://www.usnews.com/news/education-news/articles/2017-05-09/black-girls-are-twice-as-likely-to-be-suspended-in-every-state.

28. Bonilla-Silva has pointed out that "race and gender are infused within the emotional repository" of those who are racialized within unequal systems. Bonilla-Silva, "Feeling Race," 2.

29. Cooley contends that we use how others view our performance to create the social meaning of our behavior. Charles Cooley, "The Looking-Glass Self," in *Symbolic Interaction*, ed. J. Manis and A. Meltzer (Boston: Allyn & Bacon, 1972), 231–33.

30. W. E. B. Du Bois, *The Souls of Black Folks* (New York: Bantam, 1989, originally published in 1903), 1–2.

31. Ruth Wilson Gilmore, *Golden Gulag: Prisons, Surplus, Crisis, and Opposition in Globalizing California* (Berkeley: University of California Press, 2007), 242.

32. Regina Bradley, *Chronicling Stankonia: The Rise of the Hip-hop South* (Chapel Hill: University of North Carolina Press, 2021), 81; B. Brian Foster, *I Don't Like the Blues: Race, Place, and the Backbeat of Black Life* (Chapel Hill: UNC Press Books, 2020), 44–45.

33. The argument here is that Black people live within a territory governed by politically inscribed practices that perpetuate anti-Blackness, with subterritories that in part shape the texture of those anti-Black practices. Marcus Anthony Hunter and Zandria Robinson, *Chocolate Cities: The Black Map of American Life* (Berkeley: University of California Press, 2018), 4–5.

34. Hunter and Robinson, *Chocolate Cities*, 2.

35. Isoke works with and through Hortense Spillers's work to suggest that Black ethnographers that work in Black space using Black logics are working through a cultural field that is cast away as unwanted debris irrelevant to empirical understandings of knowing, space, and place. Zenzele Isoke, "Black Ethnography, Black (Female) Aesthetics: Thinking/Writing/Saying/Sounding Black Political Life," *Theory & Event* 21, no. 1 (2018): 152–53, 152, https://muse.jhu.edu/issue/37987.

36. Zandria F. Robinson, *This Ain't Chicago: Race, Class, and Regional Identity in the Post-Soul South* (Chapel Hill: UNC Press Books, 2014), 7.

37. Christina Sharpe, *In the Wake: On Blackness and Being* (Durham, NC: Duke University Press, 2016), 14.

38. Sharpe in *In the Wake* talks about the violence of abstraction, and I am using it here to point to the ways grounding theory in lived experiences allows us to see the ways it unfolds in the world. Patricia J. Saunders, "Fugitive Dreams of Diaspora: Conversations with Saidiya Hartman," *Anthurium: A Caribbean Studies Journal* 6, no. 1 (2008): 7, https://anthurium.miami.edu/articles/abstract/10.33596/anth.115/.

39. Kevin Quashie, *The Sovereignty of Quiet: Beyond Resistance in Black Culture* (New Brunswick, NJ: Rutgers University Press, 2012), 4.

40. "Trap" is a southern usage that means to sell drugs.

41. Perry, *South to America*, 136.

42. Richard Iton, *In Search of the Black Fantastic: Politics & Popular Culture in the Post—Civil Rights Era* (Oxford: Oxford University Press, 2010), 11.

43. Iton, *In Search of the Black Fantastic*, 11.

44. Paso, "Outro," *Emotional Pain* [Album].

45. Authenticity locks us into scripts and binary modes of relations, while sincerity gets to that something-elseness of being and race to allow us to think about how certain styles and performances feel Black through the ways they point to Black interiority and its movement. John L. Jackson Jr., *Real Black: Adventures in Racial Sincerity* (Chicago: University of Chicago Press, 2005), 15–16.

46. Sara Ahmed calls this the "emotionality of texts." Sara Ahmed, *Cultural Politics of Emotion* (Edinburgh: University of Edinburgh Press, 2004), 13.

47. This is a shoutout to Rod Wave's song "Don't Forget."

48. Tennille Nicole Allen and Antonia Randolph, "Listening for the Interior in Hip-hop and R&B Music," *Sociology of Race and Ethnicity* 6, no. 1 (2020): 50, https://doi.org/10.1177/2332649219866470.

49. bell hooks documents this process in "An Aesthetic of Blackness: Strange and Oppositional," *Lenox Avenue: A Journal of Interarts Inquiry* 1 (1995): 65–66, https://doi.org/10.2307/4177045.

50. Christina Sharpe, "Beauty Is a Method," *E-flux* 105 (2019), https://www.e-flux.com/journal/105/303916/beauty-is-a-method/.

51. 2 Chainz, "It's a Vibe," *Pretty Girls Like Trap Music* [CD] Def Jam Recordings (2017).

52. Anthony James Williams calls upon sociologists to take up this task in "Wayward in Sociology?," *Contexts* 19, no. 4 (2020): 82.

53. Zora Neale Hurston, *Dust Tracks on a Road* (New York: Harper Perennial, 2006), 168.

CHAPTER 1: LET ME VIBE

1. US Census Bureau, "American Community Survey 5-Year Estimates," Census Reporter profile page for Weldon, NC, http://censusreporter.org/profiles/16000US3771780-weldon-nc/.

2. US Census Bureau, "Roanoke Rapids City, North Carolina," Census.gov, 2018, https://www.census.gov/quickfacts/roanokerapidscitynorthcarolina.

3. Billy Ball, "N.C. Supreme Court Weighs Who's to Blame for 'Entrenched Inequities' in Halifax County Schools," NC Policy Watch, April 16, 2018, http://pulse.ncpolicywatch.org/2018/04/16/n-c-supreme-court-weighs-whos-to-blame-for-entrenched-inequities-in-halifax-county-schools/.

4. Ruth Wilson Gilmore, *Golden Gulag: Prisons, Surplus, Crisis, and Opposition in Globalizing California* (Berkeley: University of California Press, 2007), 28.

5. Simone Browne, *Dark Matters: On the Surveillance of Blackness* (Durham, NC: Duke University Press, 2015), 12.

6. Saidiya Hartman, when she contends "that the barbarism of slavery did not express itself singularly in the constitution of the slave as object but also in the forms of subjectivity and circumscribed humanity imputed on the enslaved." Saidiya Hartman, *Scenes of Subjection: Terror, Slavery, and Self-Making in Nineteenth-Century America* (Oxford: Oxford University Press, 1997), 6.

7. Da'Shaun L. Harrison, *Belly of the Beast: The Politics of Anti-Fatness as Anti-Blackness* (Berkeley, CA: North Atlantic Books, 2021), 58.

8. Lilly Price, "Rodan + Fields Fires Woman after Alleged Assault of Black Teen at Swimming Pool," *USA Today*, July 2, 2018, https://www.usatoday.com/story/news/nation-now/2018/07/02/black-teen-assaulted-swimming-pool-rodan-fields-fires-attacker/750429002/.

9. Jessica Campisi, Emily Smith, Eric Levenson, and Kimberly Hutcherson, "After Internet Mockery, 'Permit Patty' Resigns as CEO of Cannabis-Products Company," CNN, June 26, 2018, https://www.cnn.com/2018/06/25/us/permit-patty-san-francisco-trnd/index.html.

10. Greg Childress, "State Supreme Court: Sound Education A State Responsibility," The Progressive Pulse (2018), http://pulse.ncpolicywatch.org/2018/12/27/state-supreme-court-sound-education-a-state-responsibility/.

11. Census data was compiled by Prison Policy Initiative, "Appendix A. Counties—Ratios of Overrepresentation," PrisonPolicy.org, Retrieved January 3, 2021, https://www.prisonpolicy .org/racialgeography/counties.html.

12. Melissa Boughton, "In Their Own Words: North Carolina Prisoners Share Experiences from the Inside During COVID-19 Pandemic," NC Policy Watch, April 13, 2020, http:// www.ncpolicywatch.com/2020/04/13/in-their-own-words-north-carolina-prisoners-share -experiences-from-the-inside-during-covid-19-pandemic/.

13. Kenneth Clark, "James Baldwin Interview," in *Conversations with James Baldwin*, ed. F. L. Standley and L. H. Pratt (Jackson: University Press of Mississippi, 1963), 45.

14. Robinson, *This Ain't Chicago*, 94–95.

15. Kurtyka, *Trends, Vibes, and Energies*, 7; Friedman, "Mårten Spångberg and the Vibe of Contemporaneity," 8.

16. Janine Young Kim, "Racial Emotions and the Feeling of Equality," *University of Colorado Law Review* 87 (2016): 444.

17. Rinaldo Walcott, *The Long Emancipation: Moving toward Black Freedom* (Durham, NC: Duke University Press, 2021): 11.

18. When I say "inner registers," I am thinking about affect, feeling, and emotion. These are key concepts in the affective turn within the social sciences. I develop my understanding of these terms in conversation with Deborah Gould in her contention that the definitions of these terms are not inherently real but are artificial namings whose importance lies less in the boundaries drawn between each other and more in providing a language for us to strengthen our understanding of the emotional constructing of the world. "Affect" refers to unconscious and unnamed feelings and states produced in response to relations or contacts with people or things. Gould defines affect as "the body's ongoing and relatively amorphous inventory-taking of coming into contact and interacting with the world." Affect then can be thought of as those experiences that a person's body registers but are not fully actualized in the consciousness of the person, nor are they articulated. Eric Shouse contends that a feeling is a personal sensation that is checked or negotiated against previous experiences and understandings of the world. In building on Shouse, I think of feeling as a bodily felt experience that has not taken meaning in the social world yet. Emotion, which I am linking vibe to, is affect actualized and a display of feeling. Gould builds on Geertz and writes, "An emotion brings vague bodily sensation into the realm of cultural meanings . . . is the systems of signification that structure our feelings." Similarly, Brian Massumi positions emotion as the expression of affect through language and cultural signifiers. For me, emotion is the social ordering and performance of our feelings and affective registers. Deborah B. Gould, *Moving Politics: Emotion and ACT UP's Fight against AIDS* (Chicago: University of Chicago Press, 2009), 19; Eric Shouse, "Feeling, Emotion, Affect," *M/C Journal* 8, no. 6 (2005), https:// doi.org/10.5204/mcj.2443; Brian Massumi, "Navigating Movements: An Interview with Brian Massumi," *21 C Magazine* (2003), retrieved from http://www.brianmassumi.com/interviews/ NAVIGATING%20MOVEMENTS.pdf.

19. Kim, *Racial Emotions and the Feeling of Equality*, 442.

20. Eduardo Bericat reviews the field of sociology of emotions in his article "The Sociology of Emotions: Four Decades of Progress" and states that "emotions constitute the bodily manifestation of the importance that an event in the natural or social world has for a subject."

The discipline of sociology has conceptualized emotion as a social process influenced by social acts; the person's expectations in the situation; the person's active social identity at each moment; and the subject's identification with other persons or a group. Eduardo Bericat, "The Sociology of Emotions: Four Decades of Progress," *Current Sociology* 64, no. 3 (2016): 493.

21. Du Bois, *Souls of Black Folks*, 2.

22. John Eason calls the rural South driving economies, where cars and car rides are part of the social fabric of life. Eason, *Big House on the Prairie*, 12.

23. Browne builds on Howard Winant's conceptualization of dark matter, which is a way to think about race and racism as the invisible substance that organizes the modern world and contends that anti-Blackness is the concealed medium that underpins modern uses of surveillance. Browne, *Dark Matters*, 9.

24. I am talking back to James Baldwin here.

25. Actup Bill, "Flair," YouTube, https://www.youtube.com/watch?v=KyvsneUeQRk.

26. Corey Miles, "Black Rural Feminist Trap," 45.

27. Amy C. Wilkins and Jennifer A. Pace, "Class, Race, and Emotions," in *Handbook of the Sociology of Emotions: Volume II*, ed. Jan E. Stets and Jonathan H. Turner (New York: Springer, 2014), 394–95.

28. Loïc Wacquant suggests that the criminal legal system is a race-making institution, meaning that it does not simply engage Black people differently, but rather produces racial demarcations and makes racial categories real. Wacquant, "Slavery to Mass Incarceration," 41.

29. Marc D. Perry, "Global Black Self-Fashionings: Hip Hop as Diasporic Space," *Identities: Global Studies in Culture and Power* 15, no. 6 (2008): 636, https://doi.org/10.1080/10702890802470660.

30. Stuart Hall, "Cultural Identity and Diaspora," in *Identity*, ed. J. Rutherford (London: Lawrence & Wishart, 1990), 231.

31. Hall, "Cultural Identity and Diaspora," 232.

32. Sharpe, *In the Wake*, 1.

33. Rashad Shabazz, "So High You Can't Get over It, So Low You Can't Get under It: Carceral Spatiality and Black Masculinities in the United States and South Africa," *Souls* 11, no. 3 (2009): 281–83.

34. Shabazz, "So High You Can't Get over It, So Low You Can't Get under It," 285–86.

35. Hunter and Robinson, *Chocolate Cities*, 3–4.

36. Hunter and Robinson, *Chocolate Cities*, 3.

CHAPTER 2: USE MY TEARS TO MOTIVATE

1. Ann Cvetkovich uses Saidiya Hartman's work in *Lose Your Mother* to construct a framework for Black emotional redemption where Black folks seek reparation for the past in the affective dynamics of cultural memory rather than in legal reform or state recognition. Ann Cvetkovich, "Depression Is Ordinary: Public Feelings and Saidiya Hartman's *Lose Your Mother*," *Feminist Theory* 13, no. 2 (2012): 135–36, https://doi.org/10.1177/1464700112442641.

2. "Rocky Mount, NC Crime Rates," NeighborhoodScout.com, December 17, 2020, https://www.neighborhoodscout.com/nc/rockymount/crime#:~:text=With%20a%20crime%20rate%20of,here%20is%20one%20in%2027.

3. Richard Rothstein, *The Color of Law: A Forgotten History of How Our Government Segregated America* (New York: Liveright, 2017), 2–3.

4. Bill's mother loved her community and served it during a statewide disinvestment in Black rural communities. "Othermothering" comes from: Patricia Hill Collins, "Shifting the Center: Race, Class, and Feminist Theorizing about Motherhood," in *Mothering: Ideology, Experience, and Agency*, ed. Evelyn Nakano Glenn, Grace Chang, and Linda Rennie Forcey (New York: Routledge, 2016), 58.

5. Jesse McCarthy, *Who Will Pay Reparations on My Soul? Essays* (New York: Liveright, 2021), 112.

6. Bradley, *Chronicling Stankonia*, 84.

7. Actup Bill, "Grandma Glovez," YouTube video, 3:05, July 12, 2018, https://www.youtube .com/watch?v=bfZ89ctttUE.

8. Tricia Rose, *Black Noise: Rap Music and Black Culture in Contemporary America* (Hanover, NH: Wesleyan University Press, 1994), 22.

9. Anthony B. Pinn, *Understanding and Transforming the Black Church* (Eugene, OR: Cascade Books, 2010), 6.

10. Alan Dundes, "Texture, Text and Context," *Southern Folklore Quarterly* 28 (1964): 251–53.

11. Alan Dundes, *Interpreting Folklore* (Bloomington: Indiana University Press, 1980), 22.

12. This song is called "Dear Grandma."

13. Organic intellectual in the Gramscian sense, where intellectuals articulate and construct readings of the social world using an epistemology grounded within their social location. Kate Crehan, *Gramsci's Common Sense: Inequality and Its Narratives* (Durham, NC: Duke University Press, 2016), xiii.

14. Marc Lamont Hill, *We Still Here: Pandemic, Policing Protest, and Possibility* (Chicago: Haymarket Books 2020), 3.

15. Christina Sharpe, "Beauty Is a Method," Eflux (105), https://www.e-flux.com/journal/ 105/303916/beauty-is-a-method/#:~:text=Beauty%20is%20not%20a%20luxury,the%20 love%20of%20too%20much.

16. Christopher Holmes Smith, "Method in the Madness: Exploring the Boundaries of Identity in Hip-Hop Performativity," *Social Identities* 3, no. 3 (1997): 348, https://www .tandfonline.com/doi/abs/10.1080/13504639751952.

17. Racquel Gates talks about the epistemological power of negative texts. Negative texts open possibilities for nonnormative feelings, experiences, and allegiances not possible from positive text. They tell us things positive representations can't. Racquel J. Gates, *Double Negative: The Black Image and Popular Culture* (Durham, NC: Duke University Press, 2018), 26.

18. B. Brian Foster, *I Don't Like the Blues: Race, Place, and the Backbeat of Black Life* (Chapel Hill: UNC Press Books, 2020), 44–45.

19. B. Brian Foster wrote this sentence in the edits to my manuscript. It was too beautiful not to include.

20. Ta-Nehisi Coates, *Between the World and Me* (New York: Spiegel & Grau, 2015), 68.

21. In the 1970s Black landownership was on the decline due to the emergence of agribusiness and continued discriminatory practices by the Farm Homeowners Association within the USDA. Shantara Nicole Strickland, "For the Sake of Freedom: Landownership, Education, and Memory in Halifax County, North Carolina, 1900–1960," MA Thesis, North Carolina State University, 2012, 91, https://repository.lib.ncsu.edu/handle/1840.16/8295.

22. LulZac & Mone, "Bring Em All Back" (Official Video)," YouTube video, 2:56, December 18, 2020, https://www.youtube.com/watch?v=MKT-fMDxVPI.

23. Nina Eidsheim in *The Race of Sound* attempts to engage what makes a Black voice Black. Eidsheim contends that timbre is everything except pitch, and within this subjective space there may be gestures toward something we may call Blackness. Nina Sun Eidsheim, *The Race of Sound: Listening, Timbre, and Vocality in African American Music* (Durham, NC: Duke University Press, 2019), 6.

24. Eidsheim, *Race of Sound*, 6.

25. Charles Burchell, "10 Tips for Making Your First Trap Beat," *Fly Paper*, May 27, 2019, https://flypaper.soundfly.com/produce/10-tips-for-making-your-first-trap-beat/.

26. This is a basic formula. The best producers find ways to manipulate this style to produce different vibes.

27. Sara Ahmed argues that emotion is not in either individuals or groups, but rather produces the boundaries that allow individuals and groups to be delineated. Ahmed, *Cultural Politics of Emotion*, 10.

28. Eidsheim argues that sounds are not natural, because there are no stable sounds to be known, only that which comes into articulation because of a specific material relationality. Eidsheim positions sounds as an epistemological tool that allows listeners to extrapolate an identity onto the speaker. Eidsheim, *Race of Sound*, 6.

29. Sharpe, *In the Wake*, 33.

30. The two Ls represent Long Live.

31. Forrest Stuart in his work on driller's hip-hop videos show how the videos are collective constructions of Chicago's art world. Forrest Stuart, *Ballad of the Bullet*, 45.

32. If Simone Browne is correct in that "Blackness is situated as a key site through which surveillance is practiced, narrated, and enacted," then the state always has a legal and cultural justification to make any space Black people inhabit into a carceral one. Browne, *Dark Matters*, 9.

33. I am thinking through the possibility of hip-hop laboring on behalf of community. An attempt to take what we have and make love through it. Sharpe, *In the Wake*, 19.

34. Selamawit Terrefe, "Phantasmagoria; or, The World Is a Haunted Plantation," in *Feminist Wire*, October 10, 2012, available at http://www.thefeministwire.com/2012/10/phantasmagoria//

35. Yung Mane, "June 17th," *Live from Hurley Ave 3* [CD] 1331683 Records DK (2019).

CHAPTER 3: HANGING OUT THE WINDOW WITH MY RATCHET-ASS FRIENDS

1. Rashad Shabazz calls this living in a "prisonized landscape." Rashad Shabazz, *Spatializing Blackness: Architectures of Confinement and Black Masculinity in Chicago* (Urbana: University of Illinois Press, 2015), 56–57.

2. Hartman, *Wayward Lives*, 33.

3. Dorothy Roberts, *Shattered Bonds: The Color of Child Welfare* (New York: Basic Civitas, 2002), 66.

4. Bettina L. Love, "A Ratchet Lens: Black Queer Youth, Agency, Hip Hop, and the Black Ratchet Imagination," *Educational Researcher* 46, no. 9 (2017): 539.

5. Donna Troka, "You Heard My Gun Cock: Female Agency and Aggression in Contemporary Rap Music," *African American Research Perspectives* 8, no. 2 (2002): 82–83, http://www.jstor.org/stable/2155959. Troka addresses the erasure of women in rap and how they have played a key role in shaping the genre and culture.

6. Sarah Banet-Weiser and Kate Miltner, "#MasculinitySoFragile: Culture, Structure, and Networked Misogyny," *Feminist Media Studies* 16, no. 1 (December 2015): 171, https://doi .org/10.1080/14680777.2016.1120490.

7. Brittney Cooper, *Eloquent Rage: A Black Feminist Discovers Her Superpower* (New York: St. Martin's Press, 2018), 152.

8. Perry, *South to America*, 130.

9. Mikki Kendall, *Hood Feminism: Notes from the Women That a Movement Forgot* (New York: Penguin, 2021), 137.

10. Aisha S. Durham, *Home with Hip Hop Feminism: Performances in Communication and Culture* (New York: Peter Lang), 39.

11. Diana Khong, "'Yeah, I'm in My Bag, but I'm in His Too': How Scamming Aesthetics Utilized by Black Women Rappers Undermine Existing Institutions of Gender," *Journal of Hip Hop Studies* 7, no. 1 (2020): 87.

12. Ivy Monae, "M.O.N." (Official Video), YouTube, Feb 27, 2017, https://www.youtube .com/watch?v=pT6cxZPqMhY.

13. When talking about flow, Ivy says that North Carolina's flow is pulled from New York and Atlanta sounds. She contends that North Carolina artists use these flows as a template to construct their own regional sound. She positions herself as one of the artists who is on the New York side of the spectrum.

14. Ivy Monae, "@IvyMonae Takes You behind the Scenes of the Spoken Gunz Female Cypher!," YouTube video, 4:47, December 7, 2016, https://www.youtube.com/watch?v=nqaF Tq2jfOA&feature=youtu.be&a=

15. Elaine Richardson, *Hip Hop Literacies* (New York: Routledge, 2006), 1–2.

16. Treva B. Lindsey, *America, Goddam: Violence, Black Women, and the Struggle for Justice* (Berkeley: University of California Press, 2022), 9.

17. Elaine M. Blinde, Susan L. Greendorfer, and Rebecca J. Shanker, "Differential Media Coverage of Men's and Women's Intercollegiate Basketball: Reflection of Gender Ideology," *Journal of Sport and Social Issues* 15, no. 2 (1991): 98, https://doi.org/10.1177/019372359101500201.

18. Gwendolyn D. Pough, *Check It While I Wreck It: Black Womanhood, Hip-Hop Culture, and the Public Sphere* (Lebanon, NH: Northeastern University Press, 2004), 78.

19. Pough, *Check It While I Wreck It*, 78.

20. Mark Anthony Neal, *Looking for Leroy* (New York: New York University Press, 2013), 1.

21. Kendall, *Hood Feminism*, 93.

22. Ebony "Ivy Monae" Young, "Roll in Peace (Remix)," YouTube, https://youtu.be/ IBegdVFRXkw.

23. Racquel J. Gates, *Double Negative: The Black Image and Popular Culture* (Durham, NC: Duke University Press, 2018), 26.

24. Kiese Laymon, *Heavy: An American Memoir* (Simon and Schuster, 2018), 53.

25. I call these feelings nonnormative not because they aren't normal. They are very normal feelings. But rather I am pointing to the ways that when these feelings are lived through in Black women's bodies they are treated as antithetical to any form of meaningful social knowledge.

26. Redd, "Redd Shamone x RxRazo-Cutter," YouTube, 2:56, May 31, 2021, https://www .youtube.com/watch?v=s_TuocQIpr8.

27. Articles that engage this: Victoria D. Gillon, "The Killing of an 'Angry Black Woman': Sandra Bland and the Politics of Respectability," Eddie Mabry Diversity Award (2016), https:// digitalcommons.augustana.edu/cgi/viewcontent.cgi?article=1008&context=mabryaward; and Tamara Nelson, Esteban V. Cardemil, and Camille T. Adeoye, "Rethinking Strength: Black Women's Perceptions of the "Strong Black Woman" Role," *Psychology of Women Quarterly* 40, no. 4 (2016): 551–63, https://journals.sagepub.com/doi/10.1177/0361684316646716.

28. Jeffrey Q. McCune Jr. "The Queerness of Blackness," *QED: A Journal in GLBTQ Worldmaking* 2, no. 2 (2015): 173.

29. Durell M. Callier, "Living in C Minor: Reflections on the Melodies of Blackness, Queerness, and Masculinity," *Qualitative Inquiry* 22, no. 10 (2016): 790.

30. Callier, "Living in C Minor," 790.

31. Eason, *Big House on the Prairie*, 12.

32. A key assumption of Western bureaucratic thought is that rationalism keeps order and allows society to work. Here, I see Black aesthetics as a space to both reimage what rational is and call its validity into question. Don Handelman, "Introduction: The Idea of Bureaucratic Organization," *Social Analysis: The International Journal of Social and Cultural Practice*, no. 9 (1981): 6, https://www.jstor.org/stable/23159536.

33. Derek Iwamoto, "Tupac Shakur: Understanding the Identity Formation of Hyper-Masculinity of a Popular Hip-Hop Artist," *Black Scholar* 33, no. 2 (Summer 2003): 46, https:// doi.org/10.1080/00064246.2003.11413215.

34. W. DeVaughn, "Be Thankful for What You Got," Roxbury Records (1974).

35. David Drake, "The 50 Best Future Songs" Complex (2018), https://www.complex.com/ music/the-best-future-songs/.

36. Rose, *Black Noise*, xiv.

37. bell hooks, *We Real Cool: Black Men and Masculinity* (New York: Routledge, 2004), ix–x.

38. Mark Anthony Neal, *New Black Man* (New York: Routledge, 2015), 24.

39. Evelynn M. Hammonds, "Black (W)holes and the Geometry of Black Female Sexuality," in *Feminism Meets Queer Theory*, ed. Elizabeth Weed and Naomi Schor (Bloomington: Indiana University Press, 1997), 152.

40. Katherine McKittrick, *Demonic Grounds: Black Women and the Cartographies of Struggle* (Minneapolis: University of Minnesota Press, 2006), 3.

CHAPTER 4: WE TURNED A SECTION 8 APARTMENT INTO A CONDO

1. Rebecca Louise Carter, "Valued Lives in Violent Places: Black Urban Placemaking at a Civil Rights Memorial in New Orleans," *City & Society* 26, no. 2 (2014): 239–61, 242.

2. The venue is called Boat Ride, and to go to Boat Ride is referred to as riding the boat.

3. "In his bag" suggests that Chris performed well, and that this good performance was grounded in his own individual subjectivity.

4. Rinaldo Walcott, "Black Citizenship Forum: Black Intellectuals and the Violence of Citizenship," Black Agenda Review, 2021, https://www.blackagendareport.com/black -citizenship-forum-black-intellectuals-and-violence-citizenship.

5. Walcott, "Black Citizenship Forum."

6. Andrea A. Davis, *Horizon, Sea, Sound: Caribbean and African Women's Cultural Critiques of Nation* (Evanston, IL: Northwestern University Press, 2022), 6.

7. Murray Forman, *The Hood Comes First: Race, Space, and Place in Rap and Hip-hop* (Middletown, CT: Wesleyan University Press, 2002), xvii.

8. For my grandma, knowing the Word meant knowing Jesus. It meant having a worn-out Bible.

9. *The Dick Cavett Show*, "James Baldwin Discusses Racism," YouTube video, 17:08, June 24, 2020, https://www.youtube.com/watch?v=WWwOi17WHpE.

10. Hartman, *Scenes of Subjection*, 61.

11. Yung Mane, *Live from Hurley Ave 3* [CD] 1331683 Records DK (2019).

12. Forman, *Hood Comes First*, xvii.

13. Many have called into question whether racialized beings can make art for art's sake, with actor and playwright Ossie Davis in the 1990s suggesting, "Art among us Blacks has always been a statement about our condition, and therefore it has always been political." Ossie Davis and Ruby Dee, *With Ossie and Ruby: In This Life Together* (New York: Perennial, 2004), 86–87.

14. Serouj Aprahamian interrogates the history of hip-hop and contends that from its inception associating it with criminality has reflected a larger historical pattern of criminalizing the culture of working-class Black people. Serouj Aprahamian, "Hip-Hop, Gangs, and the Criminalization of African American Culture: A Critical Appraisal of Yes Yes Y'all," *Journal of Black Studies* 50, no. 3 (2019): 298, https://journals.sagepub.com/doi/abs/10.1177/0021934719833396.

15. Hartman, *Lose Your Mother*, 39.

16. Marcus Anthony Hunter, "Black Logics, Black Methods: Indigenous Timelines, Race, and Ethnography," *Sociological Perspectives* 61, no. 2 (2018): 207, https://journals.sagepub.com/doi/abs/10.1177/0731121418758646.

17. Hunter, "Black Logics, Black Methods," 62.

18. G50, "G50-Sleep (Shot By:@Rikoz Vizion)," YouTube video, 3:03, April 7, 2018, https://www.youtube.com/watch?v=9LqQ1VaM7GI.

CLOSING VERSE

1. Put weed inside a cigar to smoke.

2. Katherine McKittrick, *Dear Science and Other Stories* (Durham, NC: Duke University Press, 2020), 7.

3. Toni Morrison, *Beloved* (New York: Vintage, 2004, originally published 1987), 46.

REFERENCES

Allen, Nicole, and Antonia Randolph. "Listening for the Interior in Hip-hop and R&B Music." *Sociology of Race and Ethnicity* 6 no. 1 (2020): 46–60. https://doi.org/10.1177/2332649219866470.

Aprahamian, Serouj. "Hip-hop, Gangs, and the Criminalization of African American Culture: A Critical Appraisal of Yes Yes Y'all." *Journal of Black Studies* 50, no. 3 (2019): 298–315.

Baldwin, James. *The Fire Next Time*. New York: Dial Press, 1963.

Ball, Billy. "N.C. Supreme Court Weighs Who's to Blame for 'Entrenched Inequities' in Halifax County Schools." NC Policy Watch, April 16, 2018. http://pulse.ncpolicywatch.org/2018/04/16/n-c-supreme-court-weighs-whos-to-blame-for-entrenched-inequities-in-halifax-county-schools/.

Banet-Wesiser, Sarah, and Kate Miltner. "#MasculinitySoFragile: Culture, Structure, and Networked Misogyny." *Feminist Media Studies* 16, no. 1 (December 2015): 171–74. https://doi.org/10.1080/14680777.2016.1120490.

Bennett, A. "41 Percent of NC Towns Are Declining in Population: The Worst Are in the Northeast." *Newsobserver*, July 6, 2017, https://www.newsobserver.com/news/local/article159740514.html.

Bericat, Eduardo. "The Sociology of Emotions: Four Decades of Progress." *Current Sociology* 64, no. 3 (2016): 491–513.

Blinde, Elaine M., Susan L. Greendorfer, and Rebecca J. Shanker. "Differential Media Coverage of Men's and Women's Intercollegiate Basketball: Reflection of Gender Ideology." *Journal of Sport and Social Issues* 15, no. 2 (1991): 98–114. https://doi.org/10.1177/019372359101500201.

Bonilla-Silva, Eduardo. "Feeling Race: Theorizing the Racial Economy of Emotions." *American Sociological Review* 84, no. 1 (2019): 1–25. https://jps.library.utoronto.ca/index.php/des/article/view/22168.

Boughton, Melissa. "In Their Own Words: North Carolina Prisoners Share Experiences from the Inside during COVID-19 Pandemic." NC Policy Watch, April 13, 2020. http://www.ncpolicywatch.com/2020/04/13/in-their-own-words-north-carolina-prisoners-share-experiences-from-the-inside-during-covid-19-pandemic/.

Browne, Simone. *Dark Matters: On the Surveillance of Blackness*. Durham, DC: Duke University Press, 2015.

Burchell, Charles. "10 Tips for Making Your First Trap Beat." *Fly Paper*, May 27, 2019. https://flypaper.soundfly.com/produce/10-tips-for-making-your-first-trap-beat/.

Callier, Durell M. "Living in C Minor: Reflections on the Melodies of Blackness, Queerness, and Masculinity." *Qualitative Inquiry* 22, no. 10 (2016): 790–94.

Camera, Lauren. "Black Girls Are Twice as Likely to Be Suspended, in Every State." *US News*, May 9, 2017. https://www.usnews.com/news/education-news/articles/2017-05-09/black-girls-are-twice-as-likely-to-be-suspended-in-every-state.

Carter, Rebecca Louise. "Valued Lives in Violent Places: Black Urban Placemaking at a Civil Rights Memorial in New Orleans." *City & Society* 26, no. 2 (2014): 239–61.

Childress, Greg. "State Supreme Court: Sound Education a State Responsibility." *Progressive Pulse* (December 27, 2018). http://pulse.ncpolicywatch.org/2018/12/27/state-supreme-court-sound-education-a-state-responsibility/.

Clark, Kenneth. "James Baldwin Interview." In *Conversations with James Baldwin*, ed. Fred R. Standley and Louis H. Pratt, 45. Jackson: University Press of Mississippi, 1963.

Coates, Ta-Nehisi. *Between the World and Me*. New York: Spiegel & Grau, 2015.

Collins, Patricia Hill. "Shifting the Center: Race, Class, and Feminist Theorizing about Motherhood." In *Mothering: Ideology, Experience, and Agency*, ed. Evelyn Nakano Glenn, Grace Chang, and Linda Rennie Forcey, 45–65. New York: Routledge, 2016.

Contractor, Harin, and Spencer A. Overton. "An Introduction to the Future of Work in the Black Rural South." Joint Center for Political and Economic Studies (2020): 1–49.

Cooley, Charles. "The Looking-Glass Self." In *Symbolic Interaction*, ed. J. Manis and A. Meltzer, 231–33. Boston: Allyn & Bacon, 1972.

Crehan, Kate. *Gramsci's Common Sense: Inequality and Its Narratives*. Durham, NC: Duke University Press, 2016.

Cvetkovich, Ann. "Depression Is Ordinary: Public Feelings and Saidiya Hartman's *Lose Your Mother*." *Feminist Theory* 13, no. 2 (2012): 131–46. https://doi.org/10.1177/1464700112442641.

Davis, Andrea A. *Horizon, Sea, Sound: Caribbean and African Women's Cultural Critiques of Nation*. Evanston, IL: Northwestern University Press, 2022.

Davis, Ossie, and Ruby Dee. *With Ossie and Ruby: In This Life Together*. New York: Perennial, 2004.

DeVaughn, W. "Be Thankful for What You Got." Roxbury Records (1974).

The Dick Cavett Show. "James Baldwin Discusses Racism." YouTube video, 17:08, June 24, 2020. https://www.youtube.com/watch?v=WWwOi17WHpE.

Drake, David. "The 50 Best Future Songs." *Complex* (2018). https://www.complex.com/music/the-best-future-songs/.

Du Bois, W. E. B. *The Souls of Black Folks*. New York: Bantam, 1989. Originally published 1903.

Dundes, Alan. *Interpreting Folklore*. Bloomington: Indiana University Press, 1980.

Dundes, Alan. "Texture, Text and Context." *Southern Folklore Quarter* 28 (1964): 251–65.

Durham, Aisha S. *Home with Hip Hop Feminism: Performances in Communication and Culture*. New York: Peter Lang, 2014.

Eason, John M. *Big House on the Prairie: Rise of the Rural Ghetto and Prison Proliferation*. Chicago: University of Chicago Press, 2017.

Eidsheim, Nina Sun. *The Race of Sound: Listening, Timbre, and Vocality in African American Music*. Durham, NC: Duke University Press, 2019.

Forman, Murray. *The Hood Comes First: Race, Space, and Place in Rap and Hip-hop.* Middletown, CT: Wesleyan University Press, 2002.

Foster, B. Brian. *I Don't Like the Blues: Race, Place, and the Backbeat of Black Life.* Chapel Hill: UNC Press Books, 2020.

Friedman, Andrew. "Mårten Spångberg and the Vibe of Contemporaneity." *Theater* 44, no. 3 (2014): 5–17. https://doi.org/10.1215/01610775-2714538.

Gates, Racquel J. *Double Negative: The Black Image and Popular Culture.* Durham, NC: Duke University Press, 2018.

Gillon, Victoria. "'The Killing of an 'Angry Black Woman': Sandra Bland and the Politics of Respectability." Eddie Mabry Diversity Award (2016). https://digitalcommons.augustana .edu/cgi/viewcontent.cgi?article=1008&context=mabryaward.

Gilmore, Ruth Wilson. *Golden Gulag: Prisons, Surplus, Crisis, and Opposition in Globalizing California.* Berkeley: University of California Press, 2007.

Glaude Eddie, Jr. *Begin Again: James Baldwin's America and Its Urgent Lessons for Our Own.* New York: Crown, 2020.

Gould, Deborah B. *Moving Politics: Emotion and ACT UP's Fight against AIDS.* Chicago: University of Chicago Press, 2009.

"Greenville, NC Crime." Areavibes. https://www.areavibes.com/greenville-nc/crime/.

Hall, Stuart. "Cultural Identity and Diaspora." In *Identity*, ed. J. Rutherford, 222–37. London: Lawrence & Wishart, 1990.

Hammonds, Evelynn M. "Black (W)holes and the Geometry of Black Female Sexuality." In *Feminism Meets Queer Theory*, ed. Elizabeth Weed and Naomi Schor. Bloomington: Indiana University Press, 1997.

Handelman, Don. "Introduction: The Idea of Bureaucratic Organization." *Social Analysis: The International Journal of Social and Cultural Practice*, no. 9 (1981): 6. https://www .jstor.org/stable/23159536.

Harrison, Da'Shaun L. *Belly of the Beast: The Politics of Anti-Fatness as Anti-Blackness.* Berkeley, CA: North Atlantic Books, 2021.

Hartman, Saidiya. *Lose Your Mother: A Journey along the Atlantic Slave Route.* New York: Farrar, Straus and Giroux, 2007.

Hartman, Saidiya. *Scenes of Subjection: Terror, Slavery, and Self-Making in Nineteenth-Century America.* Oxford: Oxford University Press, 1997.

Hartman, Saidiya. *Wayward Lives, Beautiful Experiments: Intimate Histories of Social Upheaval.* New York: W. W. Norton, 2019.

Hill, Marc Lamont. *We Still Here: Pandemic, Policing Protest, and Possibility.* Chicago: Haymarket Books, 2020.

hooks, bell. "An Aesthetic of Blackness: Strange and Oppositional." *Lenox Avenue: A Journal of Interarts Inquiry* 1 (1995): 65–72. https://doi.org/10.2307/4177045.

hooks, bell. *We Real Cool: Black Men and Masculinity.* New York: Routledge, 2004.

Hunter, Marcus Anthony. "Black Logics, Black Methods: Indigenous Timelines, Race, and Ethnography." *Sociological Perspectives* 61, no. 2 (2018): 207–21. https://journals.sagepub .com/doi/abs/10.1177/0731121418758646.

Hunter, Marcus Anthony, Mary Pattillo, Zandria F. Robinson, and Keeanga-Yamahtta Taylor. "Black Placemaking: Celebration, Play, and Poetry." *Theory, Culture & Society* 33, no. 7–8 (2016): 31–56.

Hunter, Marcus Anthony, and Zandria Robinson. *Chocolate Cities: The Black Map of American Life*. Berkeley: University of California Press, 2018.

Hurston, Zora Neale. *Dust Tracks on a Road*. New York: Harper Perennial, 2006.

Hurston, Zora Neale, and Mary Helen Washington. *I Love Myself When I Am Laughing . . . and Then Again When I Am Looking Mean and Impressive: A Zora Neale Hurston Reader*. New York: Feminist Press at CUNY, 1979.

Isoke, Zenzele. "Black Ethnography, Black (Female) Aesthetics: Thinking/Writing/Saying/ Sounding Black Political Life." *Theory & Event* 21, no. 1 (2018): 148–68. https://muse.jhu .edu/issue/37987.

Iton, Richard. *In Search of the Black Fantastic: Politics & Popular Culture in the Post-Civil Rights Era*. Oxford: Oxford University Press, 2010.

Ivy Monae, "@IvyMonae "Takes You behind the Scenes of the Spoken Gunz Female Cypher!," YouTube video, 4:47, December 7, 2016. https://www.youtube.com/watch?v=nqaFTq2jf OA&feature=youtu.be&a=.

Iwamoto, Derek. "Tupac Shakur: Understanding the Identity Formation of Hyper-Masculinity of a Popular Hip-hop Artist." *Black Scholar* 33, no. 2 (Summer 2003): 44–49. https://doi .org/10.1080/00064246.2003.11413215.

Jackson Jr, John L. *Real Black: Adventures in Racial Sincerity*. Chicago: University of Chicago Press, 2005.

Kaba, Mariame. *We Do This 'til We Free Us: Abolitionist Organizing and Transforming Justice*. Chicago: Haymarket Books, 2021.

Kendall, Mikki. *Hood Feminism: Notes from the Women That a Movement Forgot*. New York: Penguin, 2021.

Khong, Diana. "'Yeah, I'm in My Bag, but I'm in His Too": How Scamming Aesthetics Utilized by Black Women Rappers Undermine Existing Institutions of Gender." *Journal of Hip Hop Studies* 7, no. 1 (2020): 87–102.

Kim, Janine Young. "Racial Emotions and the Feeling of Equality." *University of Colorado Law Review* 87 (2016): 438–500.

Kurtyka, Faith. "Trends, Vibes, and Energies: Building on Students' Strengths in Visual Composing." *Across the Disciplines: A Journal of Language, Learning, and Academic Writing* 12, no. 4 (2015). http://wac.colostate.edu/atd/performing_arts/kurtyka2015.cfm.

Laymon, Kiese. *Heavy: An American Memoir*. New York: Simon and Schuster, 2018.

Lindsey, Treva B. *America, Goddam: Violence, Black Women, and the Struggle for Justice*. Berkeley: University of California Press, 2022.

Love, Bettina L. "A Ratchet Lens: Black Queer Youth, Agency, Hip Hop, and the Black Ratchet Imagination." *Educational Researcher* 46, no. 9 (2017): 539–47.

Massumi, Brian. "Navigating Movements: An Interview with Brian Massumi." *21 C Magazine*, 2003. http://www.brianmassumi.com/interviews/NAVIGATING%20MOVEMENTS.pdf.

McCarthy, Jesse. *Who Will Pay Reparations on My Soul? Essays*. New York: Liveright, 2021.

McCune, Jeffrey Q. Jr. "The Queerness of Blackness." *QED: A Journal in GLBTQ Worldmaking* 2, no. 2 (2015): 173–76.

McKittrick, Katherine. *Dear Science and Other Stories*. Durham, NC: Duke University Press, 2020.

McKittrick, Katherine. *Demonic Grounds: Black Women and the Cartographies of Struggle*. Minneapolis: University of Minnesota Press, 2006.

McKittrick, Katherine. "Mathematics Black Life." *Black Scholar* 44, no. 2 (2014): 16–28.

Miles, Corey J. "Black Rural Feminist Trap: Stylized and Gendered Performativity in Trap Music." *Journal of Hip Hop Studies* 7, no. 1 (2020): 44–70.

Morrison, Toni. *Beloved*. New York: Vintage, 1987. Originally published 2004.

Neal, Mark Anthony. *Looking for Leroy*. New York: New York University Press, 2013.

Neal, Mark Anthony. *New Black Man*. New York: Routledge, 2015.

Nelson, Tamara Esteban V. Cardemil, and Camille T. Adeoye. "Rethinking Strength: Black Women's Perceptions of the "Strong Black Woman" Role." *Psychology of Women Quarterly* 40, no. 4 (2016): 551–63. https://journals.sagepub.com/doi/10.1177/0361684316646716.

Paso, "Outro," *Emotional Pain* [album].

Perry, Imani. *South to America: A Journey below the Mason-Dixon to Understand the Soul of a Nation*. New York: Ecco, 2022.

Perry, Marc D. "Global Black Self-Fashionings: Hip Hop as Diasporic Space." *Identities: Global Studies in Culture and Power* 15, no. 6 (2008): 635–64. https://doi.org/10.1080/10702890802470660.

Pinn, Anthony B. *Understanding and Transforming the Black Church*. Eugene, OR: Cascade Books, 2010.

Pough, Gwendolyn D. *Check It While I Wreck It: Black Womanhood, Hip-hop Culture, and the Public Sphere*. Lebanon: Northeastern University Press, 2004.

Price, Lilly. "Rodan + Fields Fires Woman after Alleged Assault of Black Teen at Swimming Pool." *USA Today*, July 2, 2018. https://www.usatoday.com/story/news/nation-now/2018/07/02/black-teen-assaulted-swimming-pool-rodan-fields-fires-attacker/750429002/.

Prison Policy Initiative. "Appendix A. Counties—Ratios of Overrepresentation." PrisonPolicy.org. https://www.prisonpolicy.org/racialgeography/counties.html.

Quashie, Kevin. *The Sovereignty of Quiet: Beyond Resistance in Black Culture*. New Brunswick, NJ: Rutgers University Press, 2012.

Richardson, Elaine. *Hip Hop Literacies*. New York: Routledge, 2006.

Roberts, Dorothy. *Shattered Bonds: The Color of Child Welfare*. New York: Basic Civitas, 2002.

Robinson, Zandria F. *This Ain't Chicago: Race, Class, and Regional Identity in the Post-Soul South*. Chapel Hill: UNC Press Books, 2014.

Rose, Tricia. *Black Noise: Rap Music and Black Culture in Contemporary America*. Hanover, NH: Wesleyan University Press, 1994.

Rothstein, Richard. *The Color of Law: A Forgotten History of How Our Government Segregated America*. New York: Liveright, 2017.

Rudinow, Joel. "Race, Ethnicity, Expressive Authenticity: Can White People Sing the Blues?" *Journal of Aesthetics and Art Criticism* 52, no. 1 (1994): 127–37.

Saunders, Patricia J. "Fugitive Dreams of Diaspora: Conversations with Saidiya Hartman." *Anthurium: A Caribbean Studies Journal* 6, no. 1 (2008): 7. https://anthurium.miami.edu/articles/abstract/10.33596/anth.115/.

Shabazz, Rashad. *Spatializing Blackness: Architectures of Confinement and Black Masculinity in Chicago*. Urbana: University of Illinois Press, 2015.

The Sentencing Project. "Incarcerated Women and Girls." Sentencing Project, November 6, 2019. https://www.sentencingproject.org/publications/incarcerated-women-and-girls/.

Shabazz, Rashad. "So High You Can't Get over It, So Low You Can't Get under It: Carceral Spatiality and Black Masculinities in the United States and South Africa." *Souls* 11, no. 3 (2009): 276–94.

Sharpe, Christina. "Beauty Is a Method." *E-flux* 105. https://www.eflux.com/journal/105/303916/beauty-is-a-method/.

Sharpe, Christina. *In the Wake: On Blackness and Being.* Durham, NC: Duke University Press, 2016.

Shouse, Eric. "Feeling, Emotion, Affect." *M/C Journal* 8, no. 6 (2005). https://doi.org/10.5204/mcj.2443.

Smith, Christopher Holmes. "Method in the Madness: Exploring the Boundaries of Identity in Hip-hop Performativity." *Social Identities* 3, no. 3 (1997): 345–74.

Strickland, Shantara Nicole. "For the Sake of Freedom: Landownership, Education, and Memory in Halifax County, North Carolina, 1900–1960." MA thesis, North Carolina State University, 2012. https://repository.lib.ncsu.edu/handle/1840.16/8295.

Stuart, Forrest. *Ballad of the Bullet.* Princeton: Princeton University Press, 2020.

Terrefe, Selamawit. "Phantasmagoria; or, the World Is a Haunted Plantation." *Feminist Wire*, October 10, 2012. Available at http://www.thefeministwire.com/2012/10/phantasmagoria/.

Tilton, Jennifer. "Race, Rage and Emotional Suspects: Ideologies of Social Mobility Confront the Racial Contours of Mass Incarceration." *Children & Society* 34, no. 4 (2020): 291–304. https://doi.org/10.1111/chso.12373.

Toosii. "Sinners Prayer." YouTube video, 3:13, September 22, 2020. https://www.youtube.com/watch?v=PURiHtbDHos.

Troka, Donna. "You Heard My Gun Cock: Female Agency and Aggression in Contemporary Rap Music." *African American Research Perspectives* 8, no. 2 (2002): 82–102. http://www.jstor.org/stable/2155959.

2 Chainz. "It's a Vibe." *Pretty Girls Like Trap Music.* [CD] Def Jam Recordings, 2017.

US Census Bureau. "American Community Survey 5-Year Estimates." Census Reporter profile page for Weldon, NC. http://censusreporter.org/profiles/16000US3771780-weldon-nc/.

US Census Bureau. "Roanoke Rapids City, North Carolina," 2018. Census.gov. https://www.census.gov/quickfacts/roanokerapidscitynorthcarolina.

Wacquant, Loïc. "Slavery to Mass Incarceration." *New Left Review* 13 (2002): 41–60.

Walcott, Rinaldo. "Black Citizenship Forum: Black Intellectuals and the Violence of Citizenship." Black Agenda Review. 2021. https://www.blackagendareport.com/black-citizenship-forum-black-intellectuals-and-violence-citizenship.

Walcott, Rinaldo. *The Long Emancipation: Moving toward Black Freedom.* Durham, NC: Duke University Press, 2021.

Wilkins, Amy C., and Jennifer A. Pace. "Class, Race, and Emotions." In *Handbook of the Sociology of Emotions*, ed. Jan E. Stets and Jonathan H. Turner, 2: 385–409. New York: Springer, 2014.

Williams, Anthony James. "Wayward in Sociology?" *Contexts* 19, no. 4 (2020): 82–83.

Yao, Xine. *Disaffected: The Cultural Politics of Unfeeling in Nineteenth-Century America.* Durham, NC: Duke University Press, 2021.

INDEX

ABOUT THE AUTHOR

Photo by Lee Loa Ray Guillory

Corey J. Miles is assistant professor of Sociology and Africana Studies at Tulane University. His work has been published in the *Journal of Hip Hop Studies*, *Cultural Studies*, and the *Howard Journal of Communication*.